Museum of Islands

Museum of Islands

New and Selected Poems

GARY MARGOLIS

BAUHAN PUBLISHING
PETERBOROUGH · NEW HAMPSHIRE
2020

ISBN: 978-0-87233-313-0

Library of Congress Cataloging-in-Publication Data

Names: Margolis, Gary, author.
Title: Museum of islands : new & selected poems / Gary Margolis.
Description: First. | Peterborough, New Hampshire : Bauhan Publishing, 2020.
Identifiers: LCCN 2020007378 (print) | LCCN 2020007379 (ebook) | ISBN 9780872333130 (trade paperback) | ISBN 9780872333147 (ebook)
Subjects: LCGFT: Poetry.
Classification: LCC PS3563.A6495 M87 2020 (print) | LCC PS3563.A6495 (ebook) | DDC 811/.54--dc23
LC record available at https://lccn.loc.gov/2020007378
LC ebook record available at https://lccn.loc.gov/2020007379

Also by Gary Margolis

Poetry
The Day We Still Stand Here
Falling Awake
Fire in the Orchard
Below the Falls
Raking the Winter Leaves: New and Selected Poems
Runner without a Number
Time Inside

Memoir
Seeing the Songs: A Poet's Journey to the Shamans in Ecuador

Book design by Kirsty Anderson
Cover Design by Henry James
Front cover painting, "Dream a Little Dream" by Anna Dibble www.annadibble.com
Photo of Gary by Tim Carey
Portrait of Gary, back cover, by Rebecca Kinkead www.rebeccakinkead.com

BAUHAN PUBLISHING LLC
PO BOX 117 PETERBOROUGH NEW HAMPSHIRE 03458
603-567-4430
WWW.BAUHANPUBLISHING.COM
MANUFACTURED IN THE UNITED STATES OF AMERICA

for Richard and Barbara Lynch

Contents

New Poems

From *Raking the Winter Leaves: New and Selected Poems* (2013)

From *Runner without a Number* (2016)

From *Time Inside* (2019)

1

2

3

4

New Poems

When Suddenly

You've been carrying a red-
winged blackbird inside
your ear. You're as far south
as she's made it, which isn't very far.
The two of you like thinking of
each other and the snow
disappearing. One day in March,
when suddenly you think
you're hearing things,
which you are.
A scraping, singing sound.
A bird trying to sing itself back
outside. Away from you.
So you can listen to her
making her first
announcement of the day.
Not that spring is here yet.
There's too much frost
to leave the ground.
And cold, breath-seeing
degrees. And a great
need to hold it off. Until
the earth is soft again.
And there's a branch warm
enough for her to light on
longer, without needing
to fly around your ear,
to see if she can fly back in.

Past the Sign

Friends and strangers
greet me on the street to report
last night's dream. Expecting, I assume,

I'll know more than they do about what this
or that means. Guessing I've read Freud's
Interpretation of Dreams or enough of Jung

to collect their unconscious with symbols
from a universal book of dreams. Truthfully,
I hope they've had a good night's sleep and don't

feel they have to tell me everything.
Personal to them and the breeze lifting
a fan of dreams. Fritz Perls, so Gestalt of him,

taught us to think of each image in a dream
as some part of ourselves. When I tell them
they can be a leaf on a maple, one of them says

that doesn't make sense. Say something
truer. Something it doesn't seem you stole
from your dream, an image you read in a book

of imaginings. I'll have to dive deep into the sky,
I say, where nothing's there to make more sense
than a bird-sparkling-fish. A string of singing

hooks. A list of all my confusing loves
I can report over time. If this street goes on
long enough over the bridge and past the sign.

God at the Buzzer

Who else do you blame,
some nights give credit to,
when credit is due?

When a season's work comes
down to the clock
counting down

to double zeros.
The basket's neon light
set to signal everything

you were waiting for is over.
It's time to walk back through
the wheel, the Garden's

ticket-taking turnstile.
Feeling like a loser.
Even though it wasn't you

who risked taking the last shot,
the seconds winding down
to zero. Remembering your

father who coached you,
saying some days losing's
all you've got.

You can feel sorry for yourself
or think God saves a seat for you
in Nosebleed Heaven.

Up there, so high, the court appears
to be a river of light.
(He didn't go so far as to say

Christ was a zebra, a referee.)
He left most everything for you
to decide what it was you needed

to believe, to not believe in.
The ball having left
the shooter's hand.

Eighteen thousand six hundred
and sixty-four fans rising,
the announcer says, as one.

Having bought their tickets.
Not knowing what it is, God knows,
is about to happen.

Scam

I'm not sure it's you calling, writing
your name across the sky.
That's not what you do, even in

my wildest dreams.
I don't believe you've been arrested
for a crime you didn't commit.

Stopping on the side of the road
to admire the wild orchards.
The sacred falls.

The trash left for the wind
to do with what it will.
Swirling it around your head

like that jewel
of a hummingbird.
You say could be mine,

if I wire you a thousand American
dollars in small bills,
tiny denominations.

God's eyes can't detect.
Can't find you living in the kingdom
of cell phones and random numbers.

One of which is the one I use,
I save for emergencies.
When I may have fallen on my walk

around my neighborhood.
Where there isn't anybody
who wouldn't know me. Send

a check or a diamond bird
to an anonymous address.
So one day I could be freed,

sent back unharmed, wearing
an orchid in my hair. Proof of
who I am, where I've been.

A Poetry of Leather

Apprentice yourself to a cobbler
and you'll never be at a loss
for verbs, my father said.

Although he used the word
shoemaker instead.
And some nights, putting me

to bed, he told me to look out
the window, to see Geppetto
trimming and stitching,

nailing and gluing heels
and soles. Where, one day,
the rubber would meet the road.

When shoes would be plastic-
made, boxed by children
in a dark room. Where

there's a pail of laces
and tongues. A row of newspaper
beds. A glass of water and a hand-

puppet to pass around, to play with
at the end of the day. A phrase
my father would use when he wanted

to hammer it home he wanted me
to have something useful to do
with my hands. Like Cancilla,

Ulizzi, and Ambrosia, all fine-
syllabled men. The last of their
leather-kind. Aproned, benched.

Rubbing shoe polish
into their hands. Bells ringing
over their doors.

Reading in the Bookstore

What better place to gather
this late Sunday afternoon
than in the children's nook

of the bookstore. A few adult
seats and floor pillows. Standing
room among the bookcases

designated, it just so happens,
for self-help and philosophy.
With the right number of shelves

for poetry. And space for what
volumes the staff picked, have been
moved by. Leaving handwritten,

passionate notes,
their recommendations.
This book saved my life.

I've never read anything like this before.
Don't be surprised if you stay up
until sunrise, sacrificing a good night's

sleep for the unexpected ending.
Now, when the little girl behind
her big book starts trying to turn

the pictures into words. And her mother
tells her to be quiet. There's an adult
trying to read his poem. To a few customers

who wandered inside. To his loyal friends,
whom he called beforehand.
So they could prepare their personal

responses. Arrange their praise like folding
chairs. Suggest he revise the title,
if there's still time.

Government of Two

You're sewing a flag
to wave above our bed.
Two stars, two stripes,
appliquéd on a field

of blue. I'm canvassing
the neighborhood
of our bedroom
for a voter's love.

Some nights it takes
two votes to confirm
our government
of two. I promised

no term limits,
when I married you,
not to mention
the unelected sky.

On nights when we're
bound to feel
there are no stars
and stripes. Nothing

we can do to save
the supreme courting
(we have stories
to confirm that),

the treasury of our minted
love. Although I don't want
to name just any department
to tie our love together. Although

Justice and Environment
wouldn't be a bad match,
to go with the Bureau
of Indian Affairs

and the Institute
of Peace. Although,
in naming these,
this poem has too much

bureaucracy already
and only a few lines
left to begin composing
an anthem's melody.

From the wind
inside the trees,
the evening grosbeak's
history.

Dog in a Poem

My friend Larry Raab assures me
mentioning a dog in a poem almost
guarantees its eventual success.

Not that it will be accepted
by a dog-less editor. Or posted
on a vet's puppies-for-sale bulletin board,

our town's Front Porch Forum.
Puppy, a word I'd rather not use.
Too childish, too sentimental,

too overused. Although a reader could
use some relief. And wants to imagine a dog
sitting behind a door, at the end

of an afternoon, when she arrives
home from work. Packages and first-class
mail in hand. The brochures

for new steak knives and diamond-studded
collars. She wouldn't mind spending
half of her paycheck on. If she could feel

more assured, in general, one of her dog
poems would find its way into the world.
Beyond her apartment door. At least

as far as her town's dog park
the select board thought to site
next to the community hospital

and a medevac landing pad.
Next to the volunteer ambulance bays.
And *wind socks*, Larry says are some

of the other words I need to consider
including in a poem mentioning a dog,
without saying whose or what breed.

Poetry of Current Events

It's likely this fact will pass too
into a reporter's confiscated
notebook.

Into weather's memory.
The clouds will recall you
keeping track

of where they've been.
Turning into one headline
and then another.

And the field you were
resting in. *Kicking back*,
a phrase used then,

to the metronome of the kick-
baler. That true dinosaur
of a square machine.

Replaced now by the perfection
of the round haybaler.
Which gathers a mowed field

into its mouth and spits it out,
one moment to the next.
Possessing the ability

to absorb the blood of voles
and men. And, in those days,
women and children.

Who arrived to retrieve
their battlefield dead. Wrap them
in newspaper, the news

of the day. And tomorrow.
When you'll awaken
to what just happened.

Refuse not to wait
to see if the fact of its story
is sweet and dry enough

for a cow to wander over
and eat it over and over
again. For you to go

to your desk of forgotten
memories, to write down
everything you can.

For Mary Oliver

That doe in the drifting snow
doesn't realize she won't be seen
in exactly the same way.

Won't be more aware than she is
now that her poet, Mary, is dead.
Mary Oliver. The deer who's likely

to be seen at the edge of the woods
in the late afternoon, scratching
the earth, the meadow that still is

below. Whose flowers are letters
to be browsed, pressed between pages.
So later, in the dead of winter,

a book can be opened.
Its perfume of words fly up
into the heart of the freezing air.

So we can remember
how seeing things, buried
and free, is how Mary saw things.

Before she walked back inside
to her desk, to write down everything
she could for us. With all

of her perfect comparisons. To bring
more of the world alive. In the moment
it takes now to recall her.

Worry Dolls

It's hard to fathom two billion years
from now. When, the study says,
our Milky Way will end up smashing

into another galaxy.
Not that it will make too much
of a difference apparently.

We'll have our Hubble's eye on it.
Between now and then.
Or a facsimile. This is one thing

you and I can cross off
our worry lists, leave those Guatemalan
worry dolls in their miniature boxes.

Before we fall asleep, we often pray
to them, make a wish. As if those
cloth dolls are stars.

Close enough and not a billion
miles from here. Believing
they hear us whispering

our love to them. My love
for you. Never in a billion years
I thought I'd feel inside the galaxy

of our room.
Never thought I was here
not to worry, inevitably.

Secret Language

My granddaughter and I agree
to pretend the music rising
from the electric piano is music

she's playing. And not a button
she's pushed for the machine
to demonstrate a New Year's Eve

concerto. An anthill of notes
running across the keyboard
under her fingers.

The music she believes
she's making all by herself.
A phrase she's determined

to have me believe. Now
that she's six and more
things are possible.

Even the language she tells me
she calls her secret language.
Beseeching me to let her

sit on my lap so she can
reach the black and white
alphabet

of the keyboard. *Beseeching*,
another word for her sweet
whining. For the feeling of ants

escaping their nest, one day
she'll be able to read
among the staves and clefs.

Recovering Vermeer's *The Concert*

Maybe the guard with the earpiece
is listening to his favorite classical
station. Or tuned in to the ninth
inning of a ball game.

And not just waiting
for his supervisor to alert him
I look suspicious, lingering in front
of the stolen Vermeer—four paintings

in one, if you count the decorated
clavichord's cover.
As if I were remembering the night
I would've wanted to break in.

Cut the picture from its frame.
Roll it into a calendar.
To fit under my free right arm.
Walk out onto Evans Way

in full view of the Museum
of Fine Arts and the mecca
of Fenway Park. Its lights
shadows of the shadowy Fens.

Where, if I was as fortunate
as that dozing guard,
I'd have the rest of my life
to gaze at the music room's

black-and-white floor, those squares
of notes. A thief. Appearing to be
an afternoon bench-sitter. Feeding
the geese no one's supposed to feed.

Teaching Magritte to My Granddaughters

Girls, imagine an artist plants her easel
by the side of the road, here in the country.
Looking out to the hayfields and beyond
to the forest. See the frame with her painting

of the fields and the forest, in a way you can't tell
if the painting is real or the frame empty.
And what you see is really what you see
through the empty frame. The hayfields

and forest. And not the painting.
Don't worry if this sounds confusing,
too complicated. It's like waking before
school and not being able to tell if your dream

is real or not. If anyone would believe you,
if you told them what you saw
in your mind, while you thought
you were sleeping. Let me give you two

other examples. Imagine you're standing
in a museum in front of a painting,
(say, where you live in Chicago), hanging
in the Art Institute. It appears

it's a green apple as big as the room
it's posing in. With a slice of sky
showing through the thin window.
You won't know what to believe

you're seeing. A dream? A fruit
of his imagination? An image
Magritte doesn't want you to believe in?
Inviting you to ask yourself

how this can be true.
A giant apple in a small room.
A room the size of an apple.
Two possibilities living at once.

Sometimes isn't something new
strange? Like how your mother
looks like a cloud, when she wakes you.
Which isn't the other example

I was imagining, an image Magritte
never painted that I know of.
He was too busy one evening
morning, when the sun rose

like a rose and the sky was raining
moons. Too busy painting his dream
of a curved-stemmed pipe.
With the words below,

Ceci n'est pas une pipe.
How can things be and not be
at the same time, I'm expecting
you might ask.

The next time you're visiting me.
And we're out walking
by the orchards, their blossoming
blue spring smoke.

American Playbill

I was as surprised as I could be.
Sweeping around the windswept
corner in the Windy City.
Looking up at the marquee
and seeing his silhouetted hand,

index finger pointing to the night
sky. Not having guessed ahead
of time where you were taking me.
Such an adult holiday going inside
the whirlwind of the theater!

Feeling the electric amplified bass
vibrating our seats. Seeing the lights
dim, turning day into night,
for a few hours in this Sunday's
matinee. All the actors

all shades of brown skin,
in what could have been thought of
as a White play. Given our nation's
history. Of turning truth inside out
to this day. I didn't want to think about

as the music came up
from the well of the pit.
The dancers flying into their places.
The singers dancing onto
the moving stage.

And, as the story played itself out,
I kept seeing West Monroe Street,
the road we would walk out to.
That man with one leg selling
his *StreetWise* program, rattling

his can. Sitting between limousines.
Beseeching us to give what we could.
The chorus we would hear and hear
ringing in our ears, *Alexander,*
Alexander Hamilton.

I Was Living in a Poem

My friend thought to turn his horse
into a therapy horse. Certify her.
Trailer her to Addison County's

Porter Hospital, a.k.a. the University
of Vermont Porter Medical Center.
A new conglomerate.

And lead her in. As if into the winner's
circle at the Kentucky Derby.
Wearing her blanket of championship

roses. A bouquet of perfume
so strong I'd feel I could rise
from my deathbed. Unplug my breathing

tube. Eat anything I wanted to again.
I thought I was imagining things.
Hearing my nurse whinny.

Feeling her wet nose under my pierced
hand. The needles feeding me.
Until I realized it didn't matter

what anyone else thought.
If she was nosing my arm,
nearest to the door. In this case,

my left arm. Left being the side
the poet James Wright, in his poem
"A Blessing" (my favorite verse

of all time), wrote in the lines
For she has walked over to me
and nuzzled my left hand.

He might have been remembering
the night in Minnesota
he received his diagnosis.

And told his friend Robert
Bly, with whom he'd been out walking,
Just off the highway to Rochester, Minnesota.

Lines so plain I didn't know, at first,
I was living in a poem.
Where a horse could have her shoes

wrapped in blue surgical paper.
To be led into a private room
and not damage the waxed floor.

Slip or break a leg.
No one thinking
she'd have to be put down.

Lying in State

Isn't it his dog
we're drawn to,
his Labrador retriever?

Lying in the Rotunda.
Close to his flag-draped
military coffin.

Trained to stay, until
she's called to be
of service. Somehow

she knows he's still
here. And that wheelchair,
against the wall,

was his too. A trainer
thought to bring,
to let her feel less

anxious. To sense,
if called, it was her job
to sit under his shaking

hand. Which she can't
see it's her leash he's
holding, inside the metal

box. With the bone,
he told her, he'd keep
for eternity.

Over the river and through . . .

In my wife's family it's customary
before we eat to say a round
of "I appreciate . . ."
Even the youngest, who can't say

words yet, has a chance to have
the floor for the moment
it takes to realize
there are sentences waiting for her.

And crumbs for the dog.
When everyone's left the table
and headed for the nearest
couch. An afternoon of football-

watching, drifting in and out
of turkey-induced sleep.
Eyes opening and closing.
Feeling the swell of stuffing-filled

sandwiches. Later at night
which is now. When I'm standing
alone in the light of the open
refrigerator. Trying to decide

how much cranberry sauce
I can still eat. Creamed corn
and string beans. The pie
my brother-in-law hid

behind the foil-wrapped
bird, half-meat, half-bones.
And if the leftover squash,
the buttered peas appreciate

the sacrifice I'm making
for my mother- and father-
in-law to have enough to freeze—
the good son-in-law that I am.

What the Skin Feels Like

Tai-chu writes there's a poem
more ancient than his. In which
two lovers, naked as the river,
sleep with just a scarf between them.

They can wrap it around themselves
in their lovemaking.
And later sleep under it.
Tai-chu writes they're lucky

one of their fathers owned a silk
farm famous for its worms weaving
the sky into their scarves. He knew
his wife wouldn't mind,

if he designed a veil for the two
of them, and for his son and his
fiancée. His son said was his shining
stone-in-the-river. Even when

its bed dried up, late in the summer.
And it was all his son and future
daughter-in-law could do not to lie down
among the washed stones and fish

bones. Until rain spun its web
in the trees again. And love and love-
makers opened their parachutes.
Years, from the writing of that poem,

the sky, over a landscape of beaches, would be filled with. As if the air had nothing better to do. Than to silken itself. To feel what the skin feels like.

Omen

When the duck boats cross the marathon finish
line on Boylston Street in Copley Square,
across from the Public Library
and Dunkin' Donuts, the dead breathe

a sigh of relief. Paul Revere walks
his mare back to her stall.
A deacon blows out his flare
in the steeple of the Old North Church.

Speeches forget to be given in Faneuil Hall.
No new statues are rising. Or pewter bowls.
In the Fens, near Fenway Park, a curator
in the Museum of Fine Arts declares

she doesn't have to acquire another painting
for a while. And patrons seem to accept
they won't stand in front of Gardner's
stolen art. Three Rembrandts and a Vermeer.

The bronze finial of an eagle
Napoleon commissioned.
And not this duck boat–driven World Series
Commissioner's Trophy that Chris Sale, our ace

pitcher, is raising above his head.
His winning left arm strong enough
for this. But not to catch Boston's history
of flying beers. One of which nicks a flag

on the trophy. Casting it a mile away
into the tea-soaked harbor. For all of us here,
who have no choice but to take this
as next year's championship omen.

At the Roman Ruins

You have to use your human
imagination.
No roofs. No windows.

A few half-standing headless
columns. A breach
in a wall for the barbarians

to swarm in.
And what remains of those
tile shards, those half-

broken bits of
toga time. A phrase
too humorous

for the missing bones
of laborers. Say slaves
instead. Say all of

civilization's low-paid
workers. Walking around
here you have to imagine.

If not recall, the first time
you saw a robe slip
off her shoulder.

The marble goddess
appeared. Calling you
into an emperor's

room back there
by the unattended
fire.

Postponing Writing the Postseason Elegy

It isn't time to roll up the tarps,
to store them for winter.
Nor to forgo singing "Sweet

Caroline." In New England we pray
for a few more days of summer
in October. Nights when we can't

see our breaths. To feel as optimistic
as a stiff wind blowing out to left.
For the leaves to peak for a leaf-peeper

stepping off her autumn bus.
Not to have to use our useless, season-
ending prayers.

Isn't God sitting behind Pesky's
foul pole? Who grants us
a few more nights to stay up late.

For some lives to score in extra
innings. For us to cheer for hope
rounding the empty bases.

So we can cider-toast the game
that almost got away. Save
an elegy for our bearded closer.

Ruby-Throated

Suddenly you're gone as much
as you're here. My humming
dumpling. My thumb-sized

bird. The air's all that's left
of you. And a few blossoming
fall flowers. Still trying to dazzle

you back to them. My needle-
nosed dazzler. Summer's pliers.
More syringe-like, sucking a pistil's

sweet water. From the arm
of my plastic feeder I leave out
all winter. For you to remember

where to come back to. With
no memory to remind you.
Nothing on my terms. Just

something inside,
turning winter
into blossoms. Enough so

you don't mind flying
a thousand miles inside
a wind no one like me

can see. My feathered
Thumbelina. Love's distant
frequent flyer.

If It Wasn't for YouTube

But I was going to say when Truth broke in . . .
Robert Frost

If it wasn't for YouTube, I don't know how
I'd see the everyday human miracles.
Events a stranger captures

at the right place, the right time.
I don't want to mention Frost yet,
before I see what that guy's wife's cell

phone saw and saved. Her husband leaning
his ladder against a nearby birch, bending
over a stream. As if he were still a boy, Frost's

swinger-of-birches. And climbing to the nearest
body-holding branch. To inch out,
hand-over-hand, scooching himself along.

Until he was as close to the bird as he could get.
Without breaking off the thinning branch
tip. Without getting tangled up himself

and becoming useless. To the great blue heron.
Who must have flown into the net
of wind-blown, ice-knit branches. Its head

suspended now above her body, like
some other awful image, when no one had
a cell phone to record the living, swinging

truth. Pictures, archived and exposed.
Oh, how her husband lends
himself to risk. His children watching too.

As he unthreads the bird's fish-spearing beak.
And the rest of its ragged body. Released
for her phone to record. For her to post

for the rest of us waiting for a wind-flapping
miracle, downstream, where it feathers
back onto the stone-curling water.

In the seconds it takes the video
to run out. To not believe
what it's seeing.

The Vice President Visits Vermont

I feel compelled to say
I didn't vote for you.
My disclaimer. However

lame that sounds.
When I hear your motorcade
will be making its way

through Vermont
this afternoon. Near
enough to my Sperry Road

so I can tell my wife
I'm driving up
to the fire station here

in Cornwall, to sit in
my green nylon chair
in our Green Mountain

state. The flag flies
at half-staff for Senator
McCain and Aretha Franklin,

and the thinning
deer herd in November.
I don't mind I'm all alone,

word not having gotten out
completely.
My neighbors wave as they head

north to Middlebury
and beyond. The truckers blast
their metal horns. And a lone

state trooper doesn't look
my way, I'm gathering,
because it seems the news

of the vice president traveling
south on Route Thirty
was offered as a goose chase

to his real route. I'll read
later was to the homestead,
in Plymouth Notch,

of Calvin Coolidge. Whose father,
a notary, administered the oath
of office in their sitting room.

A few hours after Warren Harding
died of scandal and a heart
attack. August 2, 1923.

The country needed to feel
reassured it was the republic
it used to be. So any citizen

could set out a folding chair
in sight of the whole community.
Even here in what some call

Bernie Sanders country.
All glasses and wild white hair.
Like Frost's, I mean the hair.

I'd share with the Vice President
the poet lived summers in Ripton
in a cabin, near a cathedral

of pine trees. I'd tell him
where to go, to see the national
historic marker there

at the Homer Noble Farm.
If his Secret Service driver made the wrong
turn. And somehow his shiny, bulletproof

SUV—I'm sure it has its own name—
had to stop at the fire station.
To ask me for the right and left directions.

Late August

and the crickets leapfrog
across the fields across from the Inn.
The Inn at Bread Loaf.

An inn that isn't really an inn.
But a barn of renovated, dedicated
rooms. Graduate students of English

and then a conference of writers
live in. Writing their papers, poems
and stories. Living the lives

they dreamed of. Sleeping
on a mountain. Walking to a pond
within sight of a mountain.

Lingering at a long dining-room table.
Waiting for a bell to call them
into the Little Theater. To listen

to a chapter from a novel
they didn't know they lived in.
Remember the night John Irving

read from *The Hotel New Hampshire*?
And said there would be an intermission.
He was just getting started. We could

stay or wander out into the evening,
if we wanted. If there was another
writer, waiting in the shadow

of the mountain. If there was no one
there to begin with.
Which is as good as any place

to let a line speak as a character.
For a speaker in a poem
to speak as an author.

For us to remember the night
we lay down in a field,
bothering the singing crickets.

To the Bookstore Owner

Large and small presses.
Chapbooks. Broadsheets.
No book remaindered.

Shelved and tabled.
Even a few signed editions.
Asleep in their original dust

jackets. Poets known
and forgotten, remembered.
Reprinted. Anthology-

memorialized. In some cases
a favorite poem memorized.
And necessary. For that

young woman, my daughter,
let this line say traumatized
one night in her Maine college

library. She survived and thrives
enough to browse the alcove's
rainy afternoon, not Amazon's

on-sale poetry selection.
Instead, these full-priced, occasionally
discounted, hard- and soft-

covered, pressed and hand-printed—
would it be a mistake to write—
bookstore survivors.

Singin' in the Rain

If you were sitting in the front
row, you'd be given a plastic
poncho. To pull over your head

just before intermission.
Yet nothing for your ears
to hear the faux clap

of thunder, the *z*
of lightning. Nothing to imagine
the rain tap-dancing the stage

isn't real rain. Or at least
water that could appear it was
rain, dropping from the cloud

of the rain-making machine.
And splashing into your real
lap, over, it seems, the heads

of the musicians dry in their pit.
Accustomed, performance
after performance, to hearing

the patrons squeal at the thought
they're about to become
extras in the weather

of the theater. Those hours
you come to expect Gene
Kelly will slip onto the screen

of the stage, sliding and twirling
the handle of his umbrella.
As if the shower could last

deep into intermission.
As if you didn't believe anyone
could be this drenched in love.

Retrieving Is Such Solace

Oh, widows gathering in the town
dog park. There are hooks
for your leashes and bowls

of fresh water. Branches for
your dogs to lie under.
Sit here for as long as you want,

remembering desire, dawn
to dusk. Before the gates
close and the moon comes

down to remember. Everything
you did together. Throwing
a star across the way

for Scarlett and Ruby
to bring back.
Retrieving is such solace.

And breaking up a fight
without quarreling.
Talking with the newly

widowed. Who can't realize
what coming here,
day after day, can offer.

Shade, conversation.
And quiet. When no one else
has arrived yet.

Why I Post Poems on Facebook

Not that I don't love
the great poems
of the printed past.
Wish that I were Gutenberg's
apprentice.

Or respect the taste
and conscientiousness
of editors.
The value of a poem
returned, rejected, still

sitting on a desk
to be read. To be
passed on to another
reader.
Before it is chosen,

discarded,
selected to appear
in a journal,
a magazine concerned
with time.

Or mailed out again,
released like a homing
pigeon freed
from its coop.
Or see the importance

of living with draft
after draft, revision
upon revision, until
the best version
of a poem rises

from the ink
on the page, the key
of an antique
typewriter.
The clicks of a plastic

keyboard.
Perhaps posting is a sign
of laziness, a cavalier
attitude toward
the past. A desire,

too quickly,
to see one's name
on screen. In order
to recall
the great work of

Anonymous
and X. Perhaps,
these days, for a poet
to be her own
printing press.

Her own congress
and government, her own
version,
you may have guessed,
of democracy.

So you, my love
and my children,
can search
randomly to find me,
one night, in a biography,

online, of Johannes
Gutenberg
(see the fourth line
of this soon-to-be
revised poem).

Who never signed his name
to anything he printed.
Who loved the cold feel
of type.
Who, if he were here,

might understand
the urge to send
a poem around the world.
Before it is written.
Before it's ready to be read.

State of the Union

General Eisenhower
installed a green
on the White House lawn.
At the end of the day
he could step onto

the West Wing porch
and imagine hitting an approach
shot. See his ball fly to a flag's
pin and drain the cup.
A word rattling in our ears

from the building's current
resident. Ike, we're told, used
to tell Mamie, his wife, to put
down her drink and watch
his practice swing. Carving

the perfect air. The way
golfers do in their dreams.
And soldiers, hunkered down
in foxholes on a beach. Waiting
for D-Day to be over. For

the planes to stop their
bombing. My father voted
for Adlai Stevenson. Who
lost, he said, because he was
too smart, too effete. Who

didn't know a seven iron
from a driver. Who was likely
to carry his own bag, enjoy
a breeze sweeping off
the Potomac. Like,

let's say, Washington.
Whom Leutze painted,
we see standing
on the prow of his boat,
looking into the distance.

Eisenhower, in his State
of the Union address,
referred to as our first
great general looking
for a ball he had just hit,

as if it were our nation's
future, likely or not, to be found
at the bottom of a cup.
More often buried in the sand,
tangled in the gorse's rough.

Notes for Our Workshop

Maybe the first line will become
the last. If you live long enough
to revise the past. Some questions
are hard to ask yourself, need to be

put aside. In order to live
your life. Speaking of General
Grant, Whitman wrote, some men
survive without any art or poetry.

Notice his imaginary footnote.
Research shows this fact includes
half of our presidents but not
their wives. Two of whom,

it turns out, were believed to be men.
In their time who couldn't come out.
Who, after hours, smoked their own
cigars. They granted themselves.

Maybe it's time to become the answers
you seek. You, meaning you and I.
In all of our happy disguises. Although
I don't mean to speak for you

or how a poem never decides to turn
itself into art. To seek the presidency.
To review the troops. Some of whom
pile long hair under their gray

and blue hats. I did in 1969.
To make it appear I was going, too,
to Vietnam. Not that I'm wanting
this poem to veer to the personal.

Or have you believe I fully served.
I was sent home with an army
of other recruits. Because there were
so many men and women wanting

to return to the battle, to earn
more than they could stateside.
They were in for a lifetime.
As far as I know, I am too,

here in my life. Sitting in my
backyard, reading Whitman.
Dressed, for the occasion,
in morning's dress uniform.

Don't We Outlive Our Numbers?

The mountain ash isn't thinking of
dropping its berries yet.
It needs you and me to express

our regrets. And all
the pleasure we have
remembering autumn

afternoons
watching professional
football, letting conversation

drift from the screen and out
through the bay window. Dozing
before halftime and after.

Half-dreams of halfbacks
and clusters of ripening
orange berries. The waxwings

gather into their mouths
for themselves and us.
For our passing regrets.

Even a running back occasionally
enjoys catching a pass,
leaving it for a statistic to drop.

Don't we outlive our numbers?
A good question to ask
a waxwing, you quip.

A line in a Sunday afternoon
poem. There to be forgotten.
Which isn't as sad as it seems.

The light lengthening.
The screen brightening
love's stadium window.

Rescuing the Statue of Liberty

Maybe you flew
to the base
of her feet.

Maybe there were spikes
to climb on
we couldn't see.

Invisible wires.
Or just brute
strength you pulled

yourself up with.
The truth
of children

pacing their cages.
Sometimes we put
our bodies

where no one wants us
to be. Turning
a body into a sign.

True, the police are paid
to talk you down,
harnessed and firm.

There are days we need
to restrain ourselves.
July 4th isn't one of them.

There are laws
against what you did.
Rescuers who put

themselves at risk.
Whoever's not
guilty stand with Therese

Patricia Okoumou
and the off- and on-
duty police.

Maybe we're here
to cheer for all
of them.

Not to have to hold
our breaths
for the children

in Texas, climbing
the walls
of their cages.

Rags of Shoes

Before I'm done, I plan to walk
to Washington, playing
my fife and drum.
I'll stop for coffee
and a cinnamon bun,

town after town.
Picking up speed,
a loaded phrase.
Before lunch.
Before word gets out.

Before the army
gathers itself
against my army
of one.
I'm used to using a flag.

As a bandana
cut into forehead
strips.
Letting a few stars
show and stripes.

I've never thought
of myself
as a desecrator.
Or a long-distance
walker. Until

I can't stand it
anymore. And feel
I have to get out
of bed. Rise
to the occasion

with my musket
cane.
Ask my wife
to join me
with her walker.

Bring the dog
along. As long
as there are rivers
nearby
for the three of us

to camp by
and sing
to the moon,
a white dome.
As long as we can breathe

into the chambers
of government.
Take off our rags
of shoes.
When we get there.

The Desire to Write Poetry at Forty

My daughter writes me
after her children are asleep,
her husband away
downstairs in the rec room,

she's been finding herself
with a blank screen,
a white piece of paper.
Things on her mind

she hasn't found another way
to say yet. Without
worrying what someone
might think. Might

tell her to keep to herself.
She tells me she's just come
across Dickinson and feels
released. Although honestly,

she doesn't understand
everything she reads.
It's more the mysterious
feeling between her

and Emily, the centuries in
between two women
alone in their rooms.
Speaking to each other

in silent words.
To write a poem.
Leaving it to somebody else
to call poetry. To turn

a rough night's sleep
into a window's dream.
A phrase, she admits,
she doesn't know where

it comes from. Emily
whispers for her to
trust. To believe
she'll remember it

in the morning.
At least enough
to begin writing.
Her children stirring,

her husband climbing
the stairs to bed.
Leaves brushing the screen's
window.

Ending the War

Approaching summer,
my wife wants to call a truce
between her and the pine-

cones. Between her
and the battalion
of weeds.

If you know Wendy,
I don't have to tell you
she's not easily

discouraged.
One summer she rose
every day

before dawn and stood
with her arms
outstretched, catching

as many of them
as she could.
The ones she missed

she raked, until
her rake lost
its teeth.

As far as the weeds went,
some of them were afraid
to rise. Having heard

how determined
she is with her hands.
How she loves feeling

her knees in the dirt.
At this point in our lives
it's not unusual

for one of us to ask
what we've been thinking
of God.

You mean the earth
under my nails,
she's said more than once.

No, I mean the war
inside the mind,
where God lives.

And Frost, who wrote
Today will be the day
of what we both said.

Trying to end
the argument
between a husband and his wife,

as to which way
West-Running Brook
runs. A truce

for the marrying kind,
he might have said.
I would like to offer

to Wendy.
So, one morning
in August, she can walk

away from her fury
of pines, and catch
her breath. Can look over

to me, standing
under the shield
of the maple tree.

Stephen Hawking's Wishes

Because you don't believe
in God, I want to ask you
how you explain, or not,

this roadside turtle, large
as a frying pan, sunning herself.
There isn't a pond around,

a stream or lake. Just a swimming
pool and acres of drying
hay. And the miles it must have

taken her to cross her galaxy
of clawed-in space. I make
a shadow of myself, a kind

of eclipse, to let her know
something else is here, passing by.
She can be afraid or not.

Hold her ground or snap out.
Opening her mouth, her jaws-
of-life. Or just go on

as she is in place. Happy
and oblivious to prayer.
And where they're burying

your ashes today, among
your peers in the Abbey
of Westminster. In,

for your sake, a godless
crypt. Although, before you
left, you planned to have

a few words of yours sent,
with accompaniment,
to the black hole nearest to us,

your Earth. The place named
1A 0620-00.
Numbers, at the end, the universe

hears as O or zero.
Leaving it for time to listen
to what it needs to hear.

For this turtle to decide to stick
out her leather neck. Whether
to go or stay.

Sleep Mode

I love that country
of half-awake. Love to doze
in a rowboat tied to a dock,
feeling a slap of water,
a slow rocking.

God, my software engineer,
thought to program me
to power down, almost shut
myself off, without giving it
a second thought. I don't like

waiting for a few back-to-back
afternoons, let off from work
early, to wander into a field
in sight of a lake. To almost
hear a stream of bees

farming the goldenrod.
I'd rather close my eyes
anywhere there isn't an officer
of the state, ripping a child
from her mother and father.

It isn't against the law
of dozing to stay awake.
To go into extreme alert
mode. In this second
decade of the 21st century.

I used to hate being
such a light sleeper.
Not knowing if I was sleeping
or dozing. If what I was
dreaming I was seeing right

in front of my eyes.
A country of children
tied into a rowboat.
A screen drifting from white
to black.

Unveiling

May the veil be lifted
from your stone.
May the wind carry it

beyond all winds.
May the sun be a light
upon your darkness.

Now and for all time.
Now is the time
for silence to rise

among the living.
Forever is now
yours and mine.

In your stone's name.
In your carved dates.
In death's first breath.

"Radical Empathy"

after Isabel Wilkerson's 2018 address
to Middlebury College graduates

It's not enough, you say, to imagine
someone else's pain, what it must
feel like. Imagining still one
step removed from standing

in another's shoes, walking barefoot
on a winter street. Crawling inside
a piss-soaked sleeping bag inside
an underpass. Taking enough

time to ask how, not why,
passed-out in his delirium,
he wound up here and now,
almost asleep, next to you.

Sleep a privilege. As well
as taking time to decide
what it is you could do.
Even kissing him awake.

You could take him
to the nearest Starbucks,
wash him and his clothes
in the high-end sink.

And not just kiss his feet.
If that's what he wants too.
You have to ask him
what he needs

and the streets
that brought him here.
How he still knows
Necessity's dream

isn't a temporary cup
of brewed coffee.
Although waking up
isn't a bad start

to every day.
Listening, beyond
self-congratulating
empathy. For years

felt on avenues
of television.
You beseech us
to know, sitting here

in graduation's
wooden seats.
Wondering who
among us will wind up

sleeping in an underpass.
Who's heard enough
and decides what it is
she has to do.

Free Love

It's spring and the cows
mount each other every
which way. As if it's 1968
again, the war raging,

and the pill was made
for anyone mounting
a demonstration against
almost anything.

Like them, we gamboled
across a field
of streets. Tempting
and taunting

the police to use
their tear gas, that year's
aphrodisiac. And later
went to jail

or home to make
a privileged love.
Before we went back
to class, checked to see

how much
was left in our father-
filled bank accounts.
At least some of us

that is.
Who hadn't been fed
on grain and open-
range grass.

Who ate whatever
we could. Even
when it was smoke.
And we couldn't see

who we were bumping into.
In this case, on Elmwood
Avenue in Buffalo.
Who, at the end

of the afternoon, was ours
to go home with.
To a strange bale
of a bed. No springs

attached. To imagine
the war was all
the insurmountable love
we made.

Upon Hearing of Justice Kennedy's Retirement

My granddaughter's reading
The Diary of Anne Frank
underneath her blanket.
She heard my daughter say
they could come for us too.

Unaware her firstborn
was listening in her room.
Reading entry after entry.
And imagining where in
the house she could hide.

The basement, the attic,
a secret place behind a fake
wall. Her father thought
to build a while ago.
When there wasn't a good

reason to believe
what she was reading.
She wonders if she
and her sister will have
to sleep in the same bed

and not say a word,
when they hear boots
on the street, men talking.
When she sees her mother
and father sharing a piece

of plain bread. Going without
their pillows. For the sake
of their daughters' heads.
She's old enough to realize
she needs a private page, to write

how she feels about
what she overhears.
What mother and father
say, when they think
their mice are sound

asleep and dreaming.
About the future,
what it's becoming.
Remembering themselves
what Anne wrote

June 12, 1942:
I hope I will be able
to confide everything to you,
as I have never been able
to confide in anyone,

and I hope you will be
a great source of comfort
and support.
The moment my granddaughter
feels reading is like

talking to herself. Letting
Anne know she isn't alone.
As long as she has her pen,
a lifetime
of blank pages.

Always On

Whoever named this thing, this
speaker Alexa, forgot to check in
with me. Who might have told it,

at sixteen, I fell in love
with Alexis, one of three sisters.
Who lived in an apartment

in Brookline, Massachusetts.
And even today there are times
I say her name, to see if she's listening.

If this ear in my house is programmed
to not listen exactly. If it has enough
room to make a mistake, assume

some names sound close enough
to recall a love that hadn't been invented
yet. We wrote letters to each other.

Stood in booths, inserted coins, waited
for a dial tone, so we could say
I love you, in thirty seconds. Letting

the phone dangle in that echo
chamber. As if the operator,
who said his name was Alexander,

would take pity on us. And let us
talk free for another sixty seconds.
A moment we have to remember,

when it's easy to forget Alexa's
always listening, always on
to us, sixty years later.

Armistice

Forget the ribbons
and swords
of protocol.
Come to the come-
as-you-are

table displayed
in the field.
Quills and decanters
of wine.
Ink and blood.

Lay down the arms
inside your hearts.
Let the vireo
be your verification.
Two nations

under one canopy
of God.
Bury your anthems
and furious flags.
Trust in your own

fury.
The peace
of worry.
Sign at noon
at the bottom

of a well.
Remember
it's customary
to write
your names

in roses
and thorns.
No need
for a date.
Break as many

plentiful
rules as you can
in your
lifetimes.
Later return

to your canvas
and nylon
timely tents.
Time is a wing-
span.

Killing a bottle of wine, you said,

which got me to thinking why anyone
would say *killing* and not *finishing*.
Or *tipping it on its end*. Or *upping*,

if you were the Queen on the day
each year her swans get counted,
her pond's cellar bounty.

Even if red wine can appear
blood-red. And that's what a squad
of special ops men toast themselves

with, after they've taken down
a presumed dictator, or come back
from training in the swamp

where they've been eaten alive.
Another phrase I question
the truth of. Imagining them standing

around a banquet table, swigging
a pigskin of chianti, *killing it*,
one of them might say.

Confusing murder with pleasure.
Using a word best meant
for the battlefield and flies.

Which got me to thinking
of all the other ways to say
Aren't we happy we stayed

home tonight, the cicadas
bowing their violins
in the evening field.

The clouds tipping themselves
over and up. *Our glasses like
bells,* you said.

My Love's My SOS

My roof falls into my living
room.
The sea's surging beyond
itself.

I used to live on a street.
A body floating by
is a life
raft.

My neighbor arrives
eventually
on his Jet Ski.
I'm blind (you can speak for me).

I stepped into the sea
of my street.
I never asked for help
in my life. Until

now. I'm not asking
for your empathy.
No one's allowed to ask me
what I'm going to do next.

Next is now.
Wherever you're writing this,
my love's my SOS.
You can do more

than you're doing.
Imagining what it's like
for me and my island
country.

Ever have a sinking feeling
you can't stand
(I'm not going to say)
on your own two feet?

I'm not your Bahamian
in vacationland.
Although I need you
to think of yourself

as you and me.
Not for the moment
you have
to write this.

Think of the sky
as the roof
you once had.
Don't let anyone

tell you praying
isn't a first step.
Until a basket
on a chain lowers

God down.
Until I'm in
your arms
again.

In the Grolier Bookshop

for Ifeanyi Menkiti (1940–2019)

The owner then, Gordon Cairnie, told me
from his couch across the room,
if I had to touch a book, I had to hold it

with two hands! I was almost a boy.
Really a teenager. Who had wandered into
his all-poetry shop. I didn't

know I was a poet yet. And still quite don't.
Uncomfortable with saying that.
Having seen the photographs

of well-known writers,
above the shelves, staring down at me.
Like glistening crows. Heaney. Lowell.

Sexton. Moore. Hayden and Kinnell. Faces
I didn't have the names for.
Or one of their books,

one of their volumes, a word
that sounded better, more adult,
for who they were. Yesterday,

in the store again, fifty years later,
none of us, the living and the dead,
could guess the latest poet-owner,

Ifeanyi Menkiti, would die over
the weekend. Without shouting across
the room to us, browsing the table

of books. Looking up to the library
of photographs. Running our hands
over the hard and paper, cardboard

bindings. (Grolier actually means
an interlacing, designed binding.)
To feel if one of the books was yours

or mine. New or remaindered.
If Ifeanyi (I met him once on Bread Loaf
Mountain) was still almost here

to introduce us. As he would have done.
Seeing us as poets. Shopping for
who we were.

Pinocchio's Mouth

I wish I had a larger vocabulary,
more like my wife's, the lexicographer.
Who finds words for me I've never heard of,

never thought of using. I'm more inclined
to let certain words live where they can,
in the dark, between pages. Speaking mostly

to themselves, like puppets in various stages
of creation. Who can't wait until Geppetto
leaves for the day, leaves them alone

to their own strings and devices.
My wife's known for staying up late,
using her night-light, to read the dictionary.

Moving her lips, practicing a perfectionist's
phrasing. I'd rather she put stones in my mouth
with her tongue. Because I'm her husband

and not an impediment to understanding
she loves syllables, as much as she loves me
and etymology. Waking up in the middle

of the night and sleepwalking to that bigger
book on its music stand. Opening it
to a random page. Letting her finger

point to a word, its definition and history.
Why it came to be in the first place.
To make meaning of silence.

In one case, how the carver, Geppetto, made
his life's work putting words in
Pinocchio's mouth.

To Call the Children Out

Call the roller of Big Cigars . . .
Take from the dresser of deal . . .
"The Emperor of Ice Cream," Wallace Stevens

When I had the chance, I should have
asked the Vice President to join me.
To drive a truckload of ice cream
cartons to the frozen border.

Arriving with all the bells and whistles
we could remember. To call the children out.
Pied Pipers of dripping cones
and small white napkins.

My government caused the problem,
installing twenty-eight flavors
of dictators. Bananas. Coffee beans.
And rolled cigars. Tipping

the balance in our favor.
Lining pockets, here and there,
with chocolate sprinkles.
Wallace Stevens, that insurance poet,

never wrote history is our only
lesson. Never assured us
of anything in his poem
"The Emperor of Ice Cream."

I'd plan to read to the Vice President
on our way to the melting border.
Two men joined by nothing,
save the memories of childhood

and children and our mothers.
Mothers crawling under fences.
Standing with their suitcases
at a newsreel's railroad station.

We thanks God, too, Ortiz,

for seeing you again.
Bounding up the dugout steps.

Throwing out a first pitch.
Taking the microphone
to thanks God. Without

all your bling. Without
waving a fist to the defiant
sky. We're *tu familia,* sitting

in Fenway's stands, television-
watching. Not wanting to know
too much of tonight's backstory.

A list of organs the bullet missed.
How much weight you really lost.
What surgeries may still be needed.

At MGH or in the Dominican.
Tonight we're all in for memory.
And for one joyous moment joined

as one Red Sox Yankee fan.
God forgive us for even thinking that.
Before we try to hate each other again.

Now because of how you're back
from Heaven's Bullpen. We'd be lying
if we didn't say we want to know

what happened, how anyone could
mistake you for a minor god.
And not for who you are. More you

without all the extra bling.
One step away from stepping into
your designated batter's box.

Dropping You Off at College a Few Weeks before Rosh Hashanah

All this poem's going to ask
of you, on the first night
of the new year, is to turn
to a stranger, a friend, someone

you've lived with
at this new college for only
a few hours. And tell them
the name of your great-grandfather.

Where he was born in a village
it's likely you've never heard of.
Somewhere borders
and borders away. A phrase

that means more than it's meant
to say. Like his name
that was changed
at the border. Because it was too hard

to pronounce and spell.
Because he didn't tell you who
the war left behind. A sister?
A brother? Your great-grandmother?

Another girl he loved
as much as his view
out to the world? The world
he had to escape. Without telling

you anything more. Just this.
This poem's asking you to share
with your new roommate and a stranger
across your dormitory hall.

Who has her own forgotten stories.
Before Yom Kippur.
Before you have to atone for things
you couldn't say or know yet.

Before you were asked.
So another day, later this winter,
when the snow wants you to forget
where and who you are.

When it's so cold you may want to transfer
to another world, you'll recall
this night you told someone you barely
know, sitting in the pew

next to you. A few words about
your family. Who couldn't possibly
be here. Praying, where they live,
a few states and countries away.

That you won't feel as homesick
as they did when they left for school.
When they told you there's love
in that ache. In a name renewed.

Hyannisport

Someone forgot to tack the 911 tag
on the upstairs telephone.
So the men, in their truck, could

arrive fast enough.
No one knew enough to keep
a saving shot in the galley

on the yacht. A vial,
to bring her back.
Some days rich isn't rich

enough. The waves can't
save anyone.
How many of them are left?

Our Kennedys.
Their toothy smiles. Shocks
of hair. Girls watching

the boys roughhousing
on the lawn.
Some families are born

with needles
in their arms. Waving
flags. Enough votes

to become senators.
The *Times* says this one,
this girl, wrote about

her sadness for her school
newspaper. Hoping to be
of service. To save someone else.

Perhaps across Nantucket
Sound. Out to the island.
Where the tourists pay

a high price for scrimshaw
and local tattoos. Where
a girl is waiting tables

until closing time.
Before she goes out
for the rest of the night.

After the Lecture by the Museum's Chief of Security

I wish the detective never told us
ninety percent of art thefts take place
in broad daylight. A pair of thieves,
disguised as themselves, walk into
a museum with their ladder and stroll

over to a Rembrandt and cherry-pick it.
Drop it in a cardboard restoration box.
Carry it casually past the part-time guard,
who nods, thinking she should have known
this is the day for the Rembrandt

to be taken away, in one case, to the Sea
of Galilee. Although that painting was actually
ripped off in the middle of the night,
1:32 a.m., to be exact. The guards, duct-taped
and handcuffed to a basement pipe.

Beneath the Atrium in Isabella Gardner's dream
of a gallery. When I learned this, I wasn't
as suggestible as I am now. And prone
to taking risks. To walk through an art
detector, wearing my fake moustache

and good shoes. Walk over to where
the painting hung to look at its frame,
the blank wall. To feel
the gale listing the boat.
The disciples trying to trim the sails.

To engage Jesus, in the stern,
to save them if not himself. To stop looking
at the light in the clouds at the front
of the boat. As if it was nothing more
than Rembrandt showing the way out.

Of life? The front door of the museum?
A path later I would take? Out to the Fens.
Those men sitting on a bench, kibitzing.
Throwing crumbs to the geese and ducks,
the swans coming too close to them.

From Raking the Winter Leaves: New and Selected Poems
(2013)

To the Redwings

Go back.
It's still
too early to
be here
to bear
the coming
snow
on the stripes
of your wings,
too early to
sing from one
end of the field
to the other
end of the world.
Look
what happened
to the face
of the wind
how it burned
before it knew
what was good
for it,
how it didn't
know what
a frozen feather
is good for.
You don't have to
believe me.
You don't have to
trust only your own
instincts.

Or the reports
of another day
coming. Like
spring. Like
those five
green shoots
too far from
my door, early
risers pointing
to the late gray
sky. As if to
say *Listen*
to the song
the wind forgot
to sing. Go back
while there's still
a wing
of time.

The End of Football

No one can remember why it happened.
No one received any notice or was told
where to redeem their tickets. Stadiums
by the sea were swept in, and fields
in the Midwest returned to fields. It was
expected citizens would know how
to cheer for themselves and read silently,
expected wives wouldn't make too
much of this, but children would. Rules,
and flags that had been thrown to enforce
the rules, were forgotten and held in
the same esteem as grass clippings.
Groundskeepers rolled Astroturf back
into the laboratory, but not anything
green by its own nature.

Speaking of nature,
people spoke more of it.
Sows were redeemed and suckled their young
in their sties, secure in their own skins.
We didn't have to think of men as lions or bears
anymore, but giants and patriots were
another story. Cities became known again
for their statues and, in one case, for its
confluence of rivers. A lot of big men were
suddenly out of work, limping and searching
for new knees. Living with us now, we needed
them to help us remember why we left our
families, why we never prayed on Sunday.

At Matanzas Inlet, Florida, after Driving to Midway Airport

Even, especially and just
here, the breeze amidst
the sea roses, the roses rising
from the sand, the sand

thrown in from the sea—
you're still walking from car
to car with a rag in one hand
and roses in the other,

a sign swaying around
your neck.
BLOOMBERG OUT OF WORK
WILL WORK FOR FOOD

WILL WATER ROSES.
Here where I have to see
you camped on your island
street, under your underpass.

Some bruises bloom roses
and not enough to eat.
Some of us are streetwise,
lakeside and seaside.

With nothing between us,

save that spit of land
the natives call The Reach.
Where the wind isn't really a bench

and not enough to eat.
Where I have to remember
Matanzas means slaughter
and blood in the sand.

After School Working, Boston, 1963

Frost was dying upstairs
   in a private room. Too late

became his coming soon.
   No patient can believe

he's doomed. After school,
   I worked there, in Peter Bent

Brigham's Emergency Room.
   A teenager. An orderly.

A disordered orderly.
   A teenager really. Without

a word for doom.
   Word came down, even

to me, low boy, our poet
   was almost done. With no

words left, written on his
   tongue. With no one else

to wheel him out or in
   to his cold box, downstairs

below my reading chair.
   Where I sat waiting to be

called, to push a gurney
   to where it had to go.

Leading Me through the Common

Christ, my swan, my leading
man, come in, begin again.
I'm all in. Inside is in. Step
into my feather-wooden
boat. Float by pedaling
harder, faster. The pond is
ours to skim. Our war was
won here. Common is
commonly good. A child
is God sitting inside
between my painted wings.
No one who comes here
doesn't return to shore,
wing-wrapped, more less
than sure, lighter than
the crossing air, night-
docking, city-trumpeting.

Late Night at Meadowbrook Pavilion

The last time I inhaled I wasn't
sitting here in the Live Free
or Die state. Wasn't sitting next to

my bride listening to these
Woodstock rockers and breathing in
a graying, silver air. *Grass is*

sweeter on the other side
of the grass I can't remember anyone
saying. Isn't memory a sweet

forgettable pleasure? And remembering
where I put the keys to the car.
Or was it her heart? Forgive me

if I'm looking more at the screen
next to the stage, as if I'm in my own
high-definition living room. And not

at their actual trio onstage.
Why did Young leave them?
Already I'm imagining their encore,

thinking of the ride home and how wobbly
I've come to be standing up, leaning
on my wife, Wendy, and that song

this crowd will call them out to sing
about Judy and not her stone-cold
blue eyes. Her eyes I can still

see, smoky-blue—I'm hazarding
a guess—inside this pine-scented
New Hampshire haze.

Parading the Cup

Even Paul Revere can't stay
dead and rises to the occasion
on Tremont Street, this Tenth Day

of June in the Year of Our Lord
Two Thousand and Eleven.
Who knew we would need

his engraving.
There's still room, a place
on this rising cup,

held above our team's heads,
for their names and a puck's
winning date.

The dead know who's coming
down Tremont Street
and not won by the sea.

The only sea here is us,
the city, revered.
Two, if by land, is a must.

So my wife and I and our son
are today's Minutemen,
watching Lord Stanley's cup

trophy the air, for less than
the minute it takes to
disappear for another year.

Before it comes back
to where we are under
the scored paper, falling

like stars, under our team's
banner, Boston's black
and gold flag.

Walking with the Wild Turkeys

How would they know
they shouldn't be standing

in the middle of the road,
September 1, 2011, the first

day of school again?
Eating stones, pebbles really,

grinding the corn they
scavenged grazing across

Sparks's field. To gain more
weight than November knows

what's good for them. To
leave a few feathers for

the children to band into
headdresses, to begin to

realize they, too, are related
to First Dawn people, here

the Abenaki and Mohawk,
related to all the big questions

of our day.
How would they know I'm just

out walking, my boots scraping
the stones, which I don't mean

for them to feel is a sound they have
to run away from fast.

As if a new neighbor's child
is assigned one of their seats

in our country school. As if
they, too, could decide, no

matter how long it takes,
to walk with me to Washington.

Where my neighbors are
standing by the White House fence

putting up their best squawk,
a word I hope isn't taken wrongly.

Putting their bodies in harm's
way. So when our President looks

out his tall window, he'll see enough
to decide to stop any company from

laying their pipes across our nation's
fields, he'll know there's another way

to fuel our needs. He'll write the order
not to arrest any wild turkey walking

slowly, eating what he finds left out
for him. To clear his throat.

Sing to the children, singing
their gobbling song.

Not Taxing the Marathon

Imagine fifteen thousand runners
in front of you in the revolutionary
town of Hopkinton, Massachusetts,
on Patriots' Day, April 19th.

And the only wall between you
and Boston Harbor is more than
a marathon and a hill full of heart-
break away. Not one hill but three,

rising from tree-lined Newton
to the half-sober students of
B.C. at Chestnut Hill,
lining the race's route

with cans and jeers, cheering
you might break down, hit
the wall, those bricks
in the heart where your will

is muscle-weary. They're full
of last night's sobering
history and wobble here,
so they don't have to open

a book for a while. You might
be sicker than you thought
trying to run while looking out
to the sea of bodies making a tide

of rolling waves, oscillating,
you could say, if you could say
anything. If you weren't trying
to catch your breath, let alone those

Patriots, John Kelley and Bill
Rodgers, who finished hours
ahead of you, who are wearing,
not sitting on their laurels

and drinking beer, not tea.
Who have enough heart to wait
for you and eventually all
the revolving Kenyans to come.

Starting with Ibrahim Hussein and
Catherine Ndereba.
If the light wasn't losing itself
in the winning sea

and the police weren't waving
those students, those Eagles, back
into their dormitories. Weren't letting
cars return to their roped-off streets.

At the Derry Frost Farm

Someone keyed their name
into one of the tilting field
stones near dried-up
Hyla Brook. Someone who

wasn't afraid to ruin the wall,
to leave a few letters for the snow
to erase. How does a stone become
a stone again, he isn't here to say.

A key scratching a falling, once-
placed rock is all is said and done.
We want to think no one was here,
too, before we came, before we turned

off the major road and drove to
the other side of Derry. Alan Shepard's
side, we guessed, our first thrown man
into space. He might have said

Pitched like a moon-bruised, batted
baseball, erasing a fence.
(Here, I have to say, if we were
standing in Fenway Park,

he could have thought,
There's a city that loves its wall,
loves to throw stones
over a monster fence.)

Our Shepard astronaut found
his way down to earth through a hole
in the clouds and didn't burn.
Isn't that what a stone is for?

To scratch something on another
stone, for time to tell. So, when one
of us returns, he'll know where
he is, she'll know where she was.

Confession

I have more books than anyone could
read in a library of lifetimes.
Many are still in their fresh

jackets, their pages stitched
together by an invisible hand.
Many are written in a language,

I lie to myself, I'll take the time
to learn. Farsi and Modern
Hebrew are two coming to mind.

Most days I sit in a room where they are,
which is everywhere, and browse
their titles, worrying what they think of

a would-be-reader. Thinking, if I pulled
a century of all-nighters,
I could relieve the tension between us,

I could go freely into my book-bagged afterlife
I have to admit is a bookstore,
a church basement, as bizarre as that might

sound. Where my neighbors have been
bringing their unread books, and marking
them down, so far down, for next summer's

bazaar, it's as if they're giving them away.
As if they're carrying a bagful
of remorse for trucking them from

the happiness of their shelves,
away from their bound
and printed lives.

Suspension

for Larry Raab

Probably it's next to impossible
to ask your dream to remember
the punch-line, to restore the entire

joke just from its first few lines.
A man walked into a donkey
store . . . isn't enough some nights

to hold your head on the pillow,
not to wake your wife, to see
what she has to say, to build

the bridge that donkey is
reluctant to cross. A dream
is born to balk when it can.

And there's only so much
you can ask of yourself,
of a sleep-dreaming-joke,

so much you can expect to know,
take from that beast
for whom *burden* isn't a word

he would think of himself.
A woman walked into a dream
might be another possibility

if you aren't into donkeys,
if you don't believe everything
we see and hear, we feel, has its way

of crossing the rope bridge
between day and night, between
the first line and the last.

It's all about timing, my wife
says in her sleep, speaks
into her pillow, when I nudge her,

when she mumbles something
about *suspending . . . flickering*
flies . . . a man walking . . .

A Kind of Country

Into this neutral air
Where blind skyscrapers use
their height to proclaim . . .
"September 1, 1939," W. H. Auden

Oh bricklayers, window glazers,
steelmakers. Wire splicers, pipe
fitters.

Oh high-rise air walkers,
safety inspectors, basement dwellers,
office decorators.

Oh building builders, ground
and sky bound, saw-grinding,
midnight-oil-burning, outside,
inside September workers.

All ash-sweeping hall-sweepers,
elevator-stranded spider strands,
typing typists, receptionists
receiving.

All hands on our flag-decorated deck.
Bell, not hand-wringing.
Gardeners in the courtyard planting
willow-sweeping-sidewalk sweepers.

Oh, now forever moment's weeping
red remembering. Not just flag-
waving memory. Bricks and glass,

plastic, steel and paper-shredding.
Street-running, avenue-filling.
A kind of country lovemaking,
grave-digging miracle in
the making.

Viva Los Mineros

se abre el perfume ciego de la tierra
y como no hay caminos
no vendrá nadie, solo
la soledad que suena
con canto de campana"

The blind perfume of the earth opens,
and since there are no roads,
no one will come, only
solitude, sounding
like the singing of a bell.
Pablo Neruda

Is that Your Tube coming
for me?
Your Ladder?

Sometimes the ground
gives back what it can't hold,
even when it's me.

Maybe You'll send a cage
to raise me, to lift
my spirits.

Can I be Your Bird for as long
as it takes to keep my wings
folded? Are You my sky?

I never thought I had a prayer
inside, when the cave fell in
on me. And all I could

see were those other eyes.
Never thought I could live
inside this mountain.

For as long as it takes
to rise.
Sometimes the earth, the ground

waits as long as it can.
Before it gives up.
Before I'm given back.

Inviting the Dalai Lama to Cornwall, Vermont

Why wouldn't you want to walk down
  Sperry Road with your entourage?

See the rolled bales, a piece of their
  plastic wrap strewn like a scarf

in the field, on your tongue a *kharta,*
  a silk-white blessing. Smell

the unpicked, fallen apples
  the wind drops into our fall

syrup, a kind of honey the yellow
  jackets forget to sting.

Why wouldn't you want to
  listen to the cows lowing

in their pasture, find Belle—
  83 pierced through her ear—

standing near her barbed fence,
  gazing, not gawking

at your maroon robe, at
  the petals thrown on the path

before you, like stones
  Stu Johnson, our commissioner

of roads, grades into our road?
   Why wouldn't you want to

feel at home here, the Adirondacks
   our Himalayas, the Green Mountains

a parade of foothills really, for
   a few of the town's llamas to graze,

shadows to coax the moon over?
   Here where my neighbors and I will

learn to bring one palm to the other,
   before you arrive. Will remember

why you are here and not home
   in the snow-filled bowl of the world,

sitting in Tibet, weaving a chant,
   singing the name of your enemy.

My Annual Appeal to the Louvre

I'm appealing to you
personally, my gift,
my director, to sell one
of your priceless paintings
in your personal collection
and donate everything you
receive to the John Graham
Shelter here in Addison
County, Vermont,
where even at the end
of the year when funds
are low our homeless
residents are sitting
like models—no, disciples—
around a table full
of donated vegetables
and other goods.
Where what they are
given is not a given.
Although if you've ever
responded to an annual
appeal outside your
vintage window, you
know how your heart
is left happily unguarded
at the end of the year.
Of course, I wouldn't expect
you not to worry about setting
an impossible precedent,
year after year, and, I confess,

I'm writing the director
of the Gardner Museum
in Boston too, expecting her
to break Isabella's will
to allow the sale of her priceless
"Rape of Europa," Titian's
god-filled bull. So a city
of street people can eat.
So a boulevard can forget,
mon Dieu, it's a bed.
So there's a window
to see to our angels
of painted hills.

Raking Buddha's Leaves

And you came to the shade
of the Bodhi tree, here a maple.

To sit in the shade. To feel
the breath of your breathing.

To see your thoughts settle,
leaf by leaf. As if they had

nothing to say. As if they
weren't yours, but

the world's. What I'm
thinking, this afternoon,

raking a wind's worth
of maple leaves into

a pile for burning. What
could be called my mind.

If it weren't for the birds,
here a mouthful of cedar

waxwings, calling,
Master, our mouths are
empty.
Master, what are you

thinking?
We can't eat the leaves

of your thoughts.
We can't sit still

until we are full.
And isn't that what

the world's saying,
I think I hear the blue jay

shrieking, I think I see
in the leaves burning,

feeding the fire,
becoming what they were?

Springtime in Boston

All winter we look forward
to lounging on the couch
after dinner. No way, really,

to trumpet the beginning
of a poem. Yet the best way
I have of saying how much

we adore each other in summer,
when the evenings stretch
a few extra innings,

what we hope for tonight,
as we lie here, not knowing
what to do with our team

which hasn't found a way
to win, as May turns to June.
As you turn to me

with a look I've come
to know. *Forlorn* isn't
exactly the word,

though it's close enough
to what I'm feeling, too.
Although you wouldn't know it,

by the way I cheer us to
believe our next run is only
one hit away. If you promise

not to get up and say you have
better things to do than lie here
until October next to me.

That the garden needs weeding,
in the dark. And even our love
can take only so much losing.

What It Is We Have to Write

for the Bread Loaf Young Writers' Conference

Someone's standing before you,
holding a key to his heart.
Who sat where you're sitting,

listening to a writer speak
about writing.
Some keys are clues to the dark

and doors to the heart.
Let's start, before it gets dark.
Let's not forget this isn't

an assignment. Writing makes you
an upstart, but not here.
I've already started to say,

Don't be afraid to start again,
to erase what you thought
you wrote.

My teacher taught me to think
with chalk in my hand.
Some words rise in its dust.

Don't be surprised you feel
a lump in your throat,
when you hear what you've felt

in someone else's lines.
Be surprised as much as you can,
when you're standing in line

in the Inn, thinking of what you heard,
what you can write.
I hope it's not surprising to think

of yourself as a writer.
And that doe I suddenly see
in the back field while I'm writing,

disappears faster than a feeling.
Isn't that what the field of a page
is for? More often than not

a page is also a door into
the dark. A pen is a key.
Here's where I'm supposed

to say, *Don't keep your random*
thoughts, your dreams to yourself.
They need your page.

They need to live outside
your heart. Once I dreamt
I'd be standing here. I can't

keep that to myself.
Frost stood outside the doors.
Or I thought he did.

He used to say, *I'm going*
to say a poem to you.
And did. You're here

to say the words you brought
to someone you've never met
before. *Be amazed they understand,*

they take you to heart. Here
we can say what we think,
even if no one has ever said it.

Even if that image of a doe
isn't the way you'd express
a disappearing feeling.

In fact, I hope it's not.
In fact, I hope there isn't
a fact you wouldn't imagine

differently, you wouldn't turn
into your own beautiful
reality. Imagination isn't

a reality show. Yet it is.
Hope dances in your notebooks.
And who doesn't want to lose

some weight, without losing?
Who doesn't want to be the last
survivor, taking notes in a diamond

notebook? *Look around you,*
if you want to see a theater-full
of survival stories, a few hundred

islands. *Guess what the writer*
sitting next to you is beginning
to imagine she wants to write next.

Did I call you a writer? *Give me*
one good reason why not.
Give me all you've got in writing.

And, forgive me, I hope I haven't
forgotten to speak, for a moment,
like a jock, like a poet taking off

his cleats in a locker room.
In my school, on my team,
I couldn't tell anyone

I held a notebook next to my heart.
I couldn't say really what hurt,
my reality. I hope I'm not hiding

in the woods behind a doe.
And yet aren't the woods
where we go, sometimes,

when we want to be alone
with a clean page. Or our room.
A little-known gallery

in the city museum.
A coffee shop. A movie
theater. Anywhere you can be

alone with your loneliness.
James Wright, one of my teachers,
wrote, seeing two Indian ponies across

the road, *There is no loneliness*
like theirs. Every day I think of
what he said. I think I can love

my loneliness, when I'm sitting
next to someone in the dark, looking
at a painting that feels like it takes up

the whole room. Or when I become
aware that doe is looking at me
from her woods. Wouldn't I see

Frost in the window, if I came back
in a different season? I'm not saying
you should like what Frost wrote,

or anything, by anyone. Only that
you take a moment, say over these
few days we have together, to see

what you thought to write in lines,
poetry and prose, to see what you
made up, to make of your lives.

See what you can take home to
your own woods, even when
there are no woods nearby.

I'm not trying to take you
by surprise totally. When I say,
now (by now you know

I'm writing this), when I put
the Lakota prayer in my mouth
and pray, *Mitakuye Oyasin,*

We are all related.
Here, at Bread Loaf, in the woods
of our words. In things we keep

to ourselves and may write later.
Much, much later,
when we least expect to need

that doe standing at her door.
When there's blood in our heart
and leaves to lie down on.

When we look around and can't
find a pen, a clean piece of paper,
and fear rises like dust.

When we remember who we were
sitting next to this first conference
night, and what it is we have to write.

Packing for Eternity

There's nothing you'll need to save
for the afterlife, you won't be able
to ask for once you are there.

It's not like going to overnight camp
with a list of items to help you survive
in the woods. A duffel bag of

socks and shorts, two dress
T-shirts. Even the angels,
it was written, were sent away

in July, for a few weeks
by a lake. A few nights to sleep
under the stars without any feeling

of responsibility to think of them
as God. Even the angels,
you were told, felt homesick

for a few hours their first night
away. And cried into their pillows,
so no one could hear them

finding a way to be brave.
No one knows if it will be any
different than what you know

now. Didn't summer used to
feel like an eternity? Sleeping
under the stars a place you didn't

want to go home from?
Sometimes we make too much
of what we don't know and turn it

into a mystery. Sometimes we spend
our whole life thinking about
what's to come, making a list

of things in a million years we
wouldn't need. Like that compass
and skeleton key, that extra crown.

Raking the Winter Leaves

There should be snow by now,
ice packing the eaves, the gutters,
and not this lawn, still green, leaves

strewn, branches where drifts are used
to being. The wind's arguing again
in Washington what's causing this.

While here, in Vermont, we're used to
saying the fields are open, we're having
an open winter, like an open house,

when any weather is welcome to come
over. And we're not electing anyone
to credit, to blame our volunteering

sun. It takes a long time for the new
sun to shine native. Science is one
of our natures. Which doesn't mean

we don't have to pay attention to
what's causing us to say it's because
of you the earth is too green here,

the snow is forgotten. Because of
you I won't have you over to rake
the winter leaves the wind can sweep in.

From Runner without a Number
(2016)

Mall Walking the Dirt Road

Good morning, shopkeepers,
   unlocking your plate glass doors,
sweeping the overnight leaves.

Hello, Security, moving vagrant
   words along.
Cheers to the custodians

of stones, stone by stone.
   The deliverymen unloading
their stores, their pallets

of birds. Congrats to the American
   redstart calling again.
Redwing's amazing

diamond in the rough.
   A phrase the field uses
to describe itself.

Dew on a hay stalk,
   a jewel in a window.
This morning you can

stop on the side
   of the road to window-
shop. To catch your breath.

To see where the deer
   sleep in their emerald
beds. To find feathers

for your headdress.
   To begin walking
in circles again.

My Habit

I like to save the Sunday papers
and read them at the end
of the year. Maybe you do too.
Although neither of us has said so,

each week picking up our country's
Times, as if we were going to sit down
at home, section by section,
for the better half of an afternoon.

I wouldn't mind if one of us said more
than we do at the checkout counter,
climbing into our cars in the parking lot.
Something strange as *hello,* as to why

we have stacks of papers in our backseats.
Not saving them for mulch.
Although that's not a bad idea
the volunteers at our Co-op more

than suggest. I'd tell them too
on December 31st I like to read
who's still married, what our world
leaders, month after month, are leading

us to. If the war was won, lost,
or changed its name.
Whose obituary was written six months ago.
I like to guess what's been invented.

Whose reputation has been enhanced.
   If anyone's reading that terrific book,
reviewed in March, to get us through
   this winter's breath. And the cartoons

that are so funny they last. The one,
   I don't know if you saw it, of a rabbit
sitting on Freud's couch, telling him
   a year's worth of bunny dreams,

I hope you find amusing.
   Enough so we don't have to say
we save things to recycle, to help
   our reputations at the Co-op's

checkout counter. And not just so,
   if we sit down to talk, to offer
our names, either of us would have
   to explain why we love to read

the sports scores late. Who won
   their division, which blouse or hat
was all the rage, what couch is still
   in fashion.

At the Border

Perhaps this is the last time
the swallows will offer their wings to you.
The leaves lift their branches.

Perhaps you'll look out to the meadow
and believe it's only the meadow
you've been seeing and not the sudden deer

who appear for their own sake and yours.
The grasses and not your eyes.
Maybe you'll forget why the wind is

your breath.
How you come to be here and there
at the same time. At the heart's

border. Where love is the father
who sent his children across the water.
Where one grandfather is carrying

another. Where a stream is a string
of plastic bottles tied to a backpack.
For the long and short journey.

For a god who didn't have to believe in himself
to pray. For a flag who didn't know
how to send back a swallow.

Our Parade

Saint Patrick weaves a ring
   of snakes around his neck.
We can walk among

the stones, dance in
   Southie's fanged parade.
Patrick drinks green beer

all day, blind to what
   a priest wears, what O'Brien
swears is the prettiest man

marching. His legs are hers.
   The tap leaks foam
snakeskin.

Boston pours a curb for us
   to sit on. Until five o'clock.
The streets are swept.

Paddy is a singing wagon.
   A snake's drunk tank.
Inside we raise a fist.

To anyone who dared
   to dance. Who has a friend
to call. To bail us out.

Walking First-Years to the Frost Cabin

It's my job to take you—three Judys,
the more-than-I-can-count Jasons—

up this dirt road to the Homer Noble farm
and beyond to his cabin. Another class

of first-years newly arrived and this our school's
way of saying *Now you're here,*

dropped off from the couplets of your
parents and their lovely unpacking

worry. I know it will be hard to hear
those lines you've heard in high school

and could recite under your soon-to-be-
cried tears. Don't worry. I'll say them

twice, because memory keeps
what you need and later plays it back

to you. I've brought a recording of his
voice and ask you to listen. So you can

think he's here, giving the gone-by hay
and rusty apples their first life

again, this time in the uncanny past
of a poem. Before they left, your fathers

and mothers said *Write and call.*
That's why we've taken this walk.

So you will have something to tell them
when they ask, when each of you realizes

what this day has come to, that you are here
and they have driven themselves home.

What Monster?

A stranger tells you
  he saw it twice.

Once in his lifetime.
  Once in his afterlife.

Diving and rising. A shadow
  of an outline on the lake.

Believed some waves are real
  myths. Outside and in.

A story. Someplace
  to begin. Sitting by a lake

at twilight. Looking out.
  Half-believing what you're told.

There are guns stored under a school.
  Cannons firing inside a hold.

A fish that's really a horse.
  Stories you have to believe

you're being told.
  Amidst the smoke

and mist.
  You don't have to call

history's veil. That wisp.
   From here, a glimpse

of a shadow gliding
   across the waves,

looking back at its closing
   wake.

Runner without a Number

Some of us don't qualify to wear a number.
To pin one to our chests. To lean closer
to the starting line. To run behind

a flock of Kenyans. Beginning in Hopkinton,
the streets lined with fans and plastic
bottles, visions of finishing downtown

in Copley Square. By the church and library,
in a sea of finishers. Half-thrilled. Half
in a body's depleted shock, tinfoil-wrapped.

Having been called a Boston bandit
myself, a runner without a number, jumping
in where I belonged. Having run all winter,

I wouldn't call training here in Vermont.
Liking to half-run, half-walk. Stopping
on the paved and dirt roads to talk

with a neighbor, to pick up a strewn wrapper.
Some days to step across a ditch
to follow a set of tracks across a snow-filled,

frozen field. As far they went, as far as I could go.
Before I was meant to turn back, crossing
where I'd just been, lost enough to find the road

again. To see myself on Patriots' Day more than
twenty-six miles away, a lifetime I can't forget.
Having broken Heartbreak Hill, really three hills

in one. Running by John Kelley's ghost,
in Rita Jeptoo's draft. Past that curbside boy
handing me a drink from his thirsty backpack.

Prayer for My Parents Dropping Me Off at College

May you see me in your mirror
   as you drive away.
May you know who I am.
   As you know where I've been.
May you save my room for the days
   I'll be home, for the guest I'm becoming.
May you see me studying
   in the heart of the library.
I can tell you sometimes I plan
   not to study. Isn't the heart
its own study?
   May we still be party to each other.
You know I know how to party
   and parting is no Southern Comfort.
May you turn to each other
   for comfort. It's hard to be comfortable.
May I drive the convertible,
   when I walk down the driveway
in May? Maybe you won't be able to tell
   I've learned how to pray any day
I might want to and I can't tell you
   everything. Maybe we'll survive
a low grade and the play I'm not
   called back for, the team I don't
make. Maybe I'll fall
   in love, with whomever I see
in the mirror, that shadow walking
   by my new door.
Maybe I'll call you later.

How to Save Your City

Refuse to stay inside and not
  line your streets with yourselves,
your cobbled stones.

When the floats drive by,
  think winter is a duck boat
of flowers. Spring is one win

away. After they pass,
  run to the river.
Wait until they arrive.

Flood a bridge with your flowering
  bodies.
Drink as much tea as you can,

your votes have allowed.
  Give in to following
your senses.

Today is a day to forgo
  anything sensible.
One day to let your heart

scale fences.
  To trophy a finish line.
To expect blessings

for the wounded and dead.
   To find yourselves wearing
a ring for the ages.

Not to forget who ran by,
   who dove into the sky.
What you didn't have to save

for later. By rising early, filling
   your city with flowers.
With Boston's red confetti.

Did the Writer Mean That?

Ask what the snow means snowing
  inside the wind. What it's doing there.
I might say something strange
  about our government. How, on a tour
through the Capitol, citizens and foreign

  tourists are invited to sit in the big chair.
To pretend a vote is being taken to tax
  the wind, to cut snow from this year's budget.
To feel how next-to-nothing gets done again,
  except the snow inside the wind.

And what it means. I mean what I didn't
  know I meant. When I walk outside,
inside the wind. And I can tell you.
  So you don't have to guess how much
you mean to me. You and my government

of snow. What you'll make of me and all
  I stand for. Without casting a vote.
Without having to gather evidence
  on your own. Only imagining
what a flag represents unknowingly.

Your hand over your heart. A battle
  song. A girl in third grade. Sitting
in her classroom of snow.
  Asking what the snow means
and if that's what the writer meant.

Summer Book Sale

You too can write a book to appear
   in summer's annual St. Stephen's
Peasant Market bin. Worn thin,
   by page-turning, you could
suppose. Although there don't appear

to be any fingerprints on the cover,
   no bent pages, where a reader
may have left off, stopped reading.
   Not forever, but for the night he began
dreaming of the book he could write.

The stains he might find inside,
   from the rain, from a rich dessert.
You might imagine your reader wanted
   to leave this copy, this first and only
edition, as mint as possible. Appearing

never to have been read. Although
   isn't it better not to assume the worst,
a worst-case scenario? Better not to care
   you signed this book for your best friend.
A Peasant Market shopper is likely to see,

if she stops for a minute by the poetry
   bin. If she opens the book
to the title page, to see what you wrote
   in your hand. If she reads beyond the benefit,
the donation made in your name.

To the Nun I Sat Next to in Summer School Biology Lab

You're beautiful in your habit,
pure black and white. Who wouldn't
want to make a habit of you,

by imagining what you're like.
The maple pours gold,
if you stay up all night boiling

down its sap. And praying
you'll let me say what I feel
keeps me up at night. Gold is all

that's left of burning leaves.
That cross on your belt is crossing me.
I'd be one bead on your string

of prayers, if you'd tell me to believe
the blood of our frog is really Christ's.
That together we'll look inside

at what we're meant to see—
a body and a ghost—the answer
we'll have to know to sex,

forgive me, the dead,
if we're meaning to pass
this station's course.

Wide-Brimmed Hat

I couldn't care less if this sounds
   too country, so Kenny Chesney.
If you accuse me of trying

   to break your heart. By singing
under my breath. By remembering
   what we had. A song is a wide-

brimmed hat and cooler than shade.
   I won't promise I can keep this
to myself for as long as it takes to drink

   a warm beer. To forget an afternoon walk
might end in bed. That's what I'm hearing
   Kenny sing, breaking his voice where

it needs to be broken.
   Here in my city-bred, half-country heart.
In your detailed dream of a truck.

For the Poet Who Is Your High School English Teacher

Understand she's standing in front of you
taking attendance with lines
in her head.

Looking for possible line breaks in her
lesson plan. Don't think *enjambment*
is too big a word for you.

She doesn't. She won't talk down to you
and will have you look up what you don't
understand.

Know she won't care if you stumble
on another word instead.
In getting there. Call it the next

word in store for you.
What she found before you.
Last night. When she couldn't sleep.

When she was thinking of how
to teach how thrilling it can be
when a word takes a breath

and you find there's more than one
way to be in the world. Two
possibilities to imagine that doe

at the back of the room, how she
escaped the woods
to be here with you. How none

of you thought to bring a gun
to school. How your teacher believed
you could write a poem to her.

Let There Be No Other Word

You're our president,
Ms. Angelou. We're writing
an inaugural for you.
Saying what the heart knows,

not knew. America feels
you are beautiful-smoke-
blossoming. A page
in a cloud's book.

Everything you wrote
you wrote by heart.
And down to earth.
Here's where we live,

you said for us.
And stood up for the carpenter
who built this stage,
standing where you stood.

Your right hand on the book
the elected raised.
Let there be no other word
for *Praise*.

Yehuda Amichai and Us

It didn't snow last night
as much as it did
the night Mr. Amichai

walked up three flights.
To read his poems to three
of us who skied across

our college's main road
to come out that night.
He was Israel's greatest living

poet. So great he read
to the world, to three of us
who poled out onto the drifting

road. I didn't know much
about him or why he drove
in a storm to find himself with us.

One Christian, two Jewish boys, shaking
snow from our boots and hats.
It would have been impolite not

to sit close to him and him to us
in that empty Monroe lecture hall.
Would have been rude to say

what he knew. I only spoke bar
mitzvah Hebrew and the boy
next to him was new to Christ,

wore his cross outside
his shirt, that night a *turtleneck*.
Mr. Amichai asked the name for.

So he could invent a word
in Hebrew to go with it.
He could fly with back to Tel Aviv.

If the plows would
find a way out of their
snowed-in predicament.

So he could drive and catch his flight.
And we could reach our classes.
Although the four of us stayed up

most of that night, shoulder-
to-shoulder, saying words
we couldn't translate, making them

up as we went. Imagining the day
we'd walk down a street,
arm in arm with our enemies.

Shalane Tells Anderson on National Television

Shalane tells Anderson on national television
she was pissed off when the bombs ripped
Boylston Street, tore the tar up. Killed three.
Mangled two hundred and sixty-four

more-than-innocent bystanders.
And says again, this Flanagan, she was pissed off.
So quickly the network doesn't have time
to bleep her words. As if we wouldn't know

what she's saying, our hometown, Boston-bred
(you can say Marblehead instead), street-running,
Heartbreak Hill–peaking, tuned-up runner.
Our street-talking, elite girl. Who says this race

is about pain in a leading woman's legs.
And knowing when to put down the hammer.
Although in her voice, every *r* is lost
to the weathah. Endearing her to Anderson

and us, but not the terrorists. She runs on Patriots'
Day to piss off, to put them in their place.
To look into the camera, our pisser of a finisher,
to break a tape across her chest.

Reading Into Things in Our Workshop

Linda says maybe her friend Maureen meant us
to take her word this way. And not how Oscar
heard it, reading the poem to himself,

after his boyfriend called, out of the blue, saying
he wasn't sure if he could stay in the relationship,
wasn't sure what anything meant anymore.

Ciel's wondering if the use of *bitch* has something
to do with her, what she said last week,
when it was her turn to speak without thinking

too much first, when she was just saying
what she felt, what came to her. Before Maureen
gave her a look. And comments began to fly

around the room, turning trash talk into
art. A form, no kidding, Arthur thought came
into being in this workshop. When it was his turn

to read what he brought, Art passed out a blank
sheet, so everyone could say what a heart says.
Which is a bitch to get right this afternoon,

when Richard, Oscar's lover, we learned a few classes
ago, walks into the room. Holding his revision
like a broken arrow. Saying he's sorry for being

later than he thought. He was sitting in his car
in the parking lot, trying to find words that hurt less,
that could be taken back.

By the Peace Bridge

One minute we're making love.
   And a man in a suit finds
himself on the moon.

Its time has come to be explored.
   Soon, you say, *there'll be a bed
on Mars, a place for us to kiss.*

Not now, I think, in 1969.
   When we learn to exist.
By looking at the stars first.

We can march in the streets.
   We can stake our bodies
where we're told it's against

the law. To make love anywhere.
   On earth. Next to a river on fire.
By the Peace Bridge.

For Galway Kinnell at the Statehouse

Under Washington, his portrait,
   in this chamber, the well
of the House, we've come
   to honor one of ours.

Word-neighbor. Poem-maker.
   Champion of using *is*
three times rightly,
   consecutively in a verse's

line. Here, where our state's once
   governor welcomes us, asks
what our state would be, if we, well-
   sitting poets, were voted in

to cast our votes. We're sitting
   at their desks with the *aye* and *nay*
switch at hand. Listening
   to his words read back to him.

By our poetry's representatives.
   His writing, singing heirs.
Who, as Frost said, *say* his poems
   into our listening air. Our poet,

sitting among us, holding his hand to his ear,
   speaker-like. Although you can be sure
he can read their lips, for a scent
   of bear, love-moaning from a bedroom,

a field's lipstick of blueberries.
   As well as for the pause between words.
Where he lives, too. In our fortunate
   Vermont. We can fill a well with the songs

of Galway Kinnell. Who we can't do without.
   Who's not here to sit for his portrait.
Who still speaks inside and out. Who rises
   to our long standing applause.

From Time Inside
(2019)

1

I make a tree inside my cell

and hang some paper bells I cut
from memory. The angel I'm
to believe is inside me.

Even with men raving
on my block, using a kind
of gangster, reindeer talk.

I give myself everything
I can receive. Nothing
that could pass through

a metal memory. Randomly
I guess today will be my day
to be strip-searched. To have

my cell tree-tossed. So the bells
can think they're ringing
for me and the angel on my block.

Dressed in snowing, everyday green.
I make a manger in my cell,
my paper room. And light a match

to bring the wise men in. To celebrate
my loneliness. To see a ribbon's
twisting smoke.

Applying to Volunteer

In the third stanza you'll hear
your fingerprints rejected.
Ink doesn't like smooth skin,

citizens who want to
volunteer. No matter how many
times you're told to go home

and return, to scrape your hands.
So the ink will take.
A poem doesn't know how many lines

it takes to do its work, to be taken in.
In an inmate's heart.
It can take a lifetime to write

a sentence in a cellblock.
You're told, in volunteer training,
once you're inside, not to look

down, to gaze straight ahead.
Show no fear of rejection by the state
of these men. From time to time,

to let your fingers bleed.
So the next time you need to have
your prints taken,

the ink will take what you did
for work. Why the officer told you
to hold your hands palms-down.

Taking the Wrong Picture

Not that I wasn't told
ahead of time.
Or hadn't agreed
to the ground rules, the spoken,

written warnings.
Couldn't guess there are cameras,
like nests, in the nearby trees.
Trained men to report

my wrongdoing, innocent
shutter-clicking me.
Who forgets no one is supposed
to be taking pictures on these barred

grounds. Memory being
all I need.
To remember what I'm seeing—
the walls, the bars,

the towers and men. Inside,
lines and lines of them,
walking one hour
to the next, not allowed to say

anything while they're walking.
It's the rule for what they did.
This line isn't an excuse,
an explanation for the real

deeds that brought them in.
These millions of locked-up writers
and readers. A few of them
who signed up for this poetry writing

workshop, sitting in a half-circle
with me. I have to remember
without any pictures. Their numbers,
their sewed-in names.

Maximum Security Pen

I agree not to bring in anything
not preapproved.
To leave my pen locked

in my car. Anything
that can be used
for spare parts.

The poem I write
in my head, thinking it can't live
on a contraband list.

I have to remember to keep
on the tip of my tongue.
That won't be detected,

scanned. A word
inside a word. Spaces
and letters. I like to keep

my word. A promise. A signed
agreement. An understanding.
Until I can't agree anymore.

It'd be dangerous
to hold my tongue. To not
write with anything I can.

A feather. A leaf. A pen
cut out of paper,
inked in blood.

Serving Time Stanzas

Let's say I'm allowed to tell you more
than my name. Which isn't as personal

as the branches losing their November leaves.
They curl, they're windswept.

Can write my address on the blackboard,
not afraid someone you know,

on the outside, will arrive at my doorstep.
Asking for anything I might do for you.

Beyond what I say in this cold, overheated
classroom, this barred school. Reading

preapproved poems. The rules of a sestina
and sonnet. What they hold inside

their sentenced lines. I don't want to compare
to the time, the bids you've done, the streets

you had to leave behind.
A judge didn't see things

the way you did. We agree you may
write in rhyme or free verse, writing

in your cell I don't have an address for,
I can't just walk to. Even if I had a leaf

with a stick for an escort. If I was allowed
to say good-bye and thank you.

How Difficult Is It?

I wouldn't have guessed
you'd love this form. And take it back
into a cell's darkness.
Even the super moon can't reach you.
Unless you dream that light
is meant for you. I mean

it's hard for me to think of so many men,
green-suited, shelves for beds, guessing
if the moonlight
will shine that far back
to you
and the super darkness.

It's darker
than I ever thought. I mean
a moon meant for you.
I never guessed
I'd be inside, this far back
inside a yard's, a wall's dark light.

Locked-in isn't a kind of light.
Although I can think of darkness
as its own light I can take back
home with me. Even if it doesn't mean
I'm here to guess
how it really is for you.

I can't know. I'm not you.
And that shining slice of light
through a cell's window, I want to guess
is the super moon giving up its darkness,
its secret, shining meaning.
So you can find your way back.

All the way back
to this poem's form for you.
So meaningful.
So darkly
full of light.
It won't leave you guessing.

When I'll come back to be with you.
Your guest. A poem turning darkness
into light.

Gated Community

Astonishing how you imagine
that *clang,* beyond the walls,
is a bell, a buoy rocking its waves.

And that shadow, a ghost
of a sailboat warned.
Meant to be following

a channel, drifting, on course.
Amazing how you hear God
in the middle of the night, *clang*

of the CO's gate, his keys,
despair's tympani. And still get up to pee
in what you call your beggar's bowl,

that cup, being what it is.
Its overflowing. An image
your poem isn't meant to escape.

The reality of where you are.
Where he's banging in your mind, a boat
of blood, your chalked-in-the-street boy.

Teaching Prison

You look at me as if I'm crazy
to want to be inside with you.
Passing a different kind of time.

Serving, a word I never hear you use.
Doing a bid is what you say.
A phrase I could speak too, wondering

if there's actually anything I have to offer,
to let time pass inside, as if it were
a regular day. *Rise and shine,* my father

would yell on his way out to work. Before
the sun rose. Before the rest of us
were awake. He never said *later*.

Short for *see you*. Not knowing how late,
most nights, he would be.
My sister and I already asleep.

My mother, bottled in, by the snowy
TV. Crazy, isn't it, how a poem finds
what it needs to believe? The rules

we can break sitting in this locked-in
classroom. Revising the lives
of our drafty lines.

Between Classes

No one's spitting spitballs
in this hall. Or talking.
Everything's against the rules,

except thinking.
Using your mind's
sentencing, the teacher-

in-me wants to say.
Imagining that shadow
on the wall's a crow,

sentenced to his own shrieking,
his own counting, counted
days. The sun setting each night

will erase. When the moon isn't
bright enough to turn a shadow
into a wall's bird. A mural.

Lighting or *alighting*, a Romantic
Period word you learn
you can use, you can take back

to your cell's crib, your nest,
your wire. Where you do
your homework, a year's worth

of assignments. Where, you could say,
you're *assigned* to live for the days
you have left inside. To hear

a crow cawing in the hallway,
the CO's admonishing,
No bird-talking. No wing-flapping.

Last Class Poetica

I could thank you for being
with me in this writing
room. For the state

letting me come in.
To read poetry, to listen to
what you've written.

In pencil. Pens forbidden.
Ballpoints use too many parts.
Ink you could tat yourself with,

draw blood.
Signs on your skin meaning
more to you and the men

on your block than me.
Although even a broken
heart, needled on your arm,

speaks to the poems
we're reading. A poet needed
to write, locked into his

feelings. Which, I'm thinking,
is why you have a key stamped
over your heart, you pull up

your shirt for me to see
as I'm leaving. To remember
you by. Poetry being

a feeling in the body,
in a cell of thoughts.
Words that can find you

later, next year,
month after month.
Where here is your life
sentence inside

this barred building
with all there is
inside.

2

Survivor's Fund

I'm donating a fall
warbler and ten thousand
dollars in honor of my daughter.

Who hasn't forgotten.
Who goes without
saying is singing, years later,

to her daughter. I'm willing,
bequeathing
ten thousand plaques

for the women
who were assaulted.
And their mothers

and fathers, who arrived
on campus
forlorn to be picking up

their daughters.
I'm pledging to look up
the name of that warbler,

the night, the time
and date she returned
to a window, the wind

her shadow. With no more
unnecessary
longing.

Call and Response

You might think it strange to hear
I like to make a sound, somewhere
between a bellow and a moan,

when I'm walking by a field of grazing
cows. Letting the note rise from someplace
I didn't know is there inside. I think might

please them to feel we've more in common
than you and I first thought. Call it
desire's stare, their big eyes and numbered

ears, my busy, empty mind. You might think
I'm making more of this than need be.
The practice of emptiness, the image

the Buddha brings. Sitting there,
eyes half-shut, half-open.
Thumb and third finger touching enough

to attend to that tender place.
So the mind can empty, the heart fill
with emptiness. Love sounds across this charging

fence. First their moans, then mine. The bellow,
the bull in my throat. The strange thought
there's more to make of our love.

For a Student Attending a Poetry Reading for the First Time

It's hard to tell what you'll hear.
Might assume was written
with a student like you in mind.

Even when the poet, between poems, says
a few words to open the door to the next poem
he's chosen to read.

When he has no way of telling what line,
or pause, might touch anyone, especially you,
in the front row. Taking notes, looking

deeply into your notebook. As if you're sitting
in a 19th-century American history class
and it's all you can do to keep up

with the names and places,
the numbers of wounded and dead.
All you can to do to wait to ask

what the poet or, you're learning, a speaker
in a poem intends. When he says
I love you like the snow clinging

to a branch. Whether he's actually speaking
for himself and, in this moment,
to you. When you thought you never

could be anything other than yourself,
reading the calendar of events and doing
what you've never done before. Wandering

into a poetry reading, as if walking
between buildings, head down to save
yourself from the driving snow. To not

have it appear you're going to a room,
a laboratory in the science center.
Where, you had read, a poet would be reading

his own poems in honor of International
Women's Day. In his own written voice.
Where, you didn't know you were hoping,

you'd be seen in this century's moment,
experimenting with a new sense of yourself—
isn't that one of the reasons to go to college?—

not taking history notes. But beginning to
write your first poem in the margin.
Thinking of words as leaves buried in snow.

See Something, Say Something

My neighbor says, in passing, he's feeling
the shift of fall to winter. In his body.
Says, it's hunting deer that gets him through

the season. In fact, he adds, some of the geese
are trapped inside their clouds and he wishes
he could pry them out. I know him well enough

to know he's not kidding. But not so well
as to ask him more without him thinking
I'm prying. Stepping beyond our friendly

neighborhood. Privacy sometimes a cloud
for what someone's really thinking.
Maybe I should call his wife. Or ask him

point-blank, I'd rather say directly, how disturbed
he's feeling. Offer to walk over to his house
beyond the trees, down his long driveway.

Anytime he hears the geese calling him.
And it might take two of us to talk them down,
to release them, to where it is they're flying.

Hive Mind–Synching

My friend, sitting outside a café
on the Left Bank, texts me she thinks
our country has lost its collective
mind. She puts down her phone
to watch the cabs and buses,

the workers walking over Pont Neuf.
I've been there once
which is enough to write
its name. And not feel I have
to text her back to defend

my life. Still living here
in the country, a half-mile
from my town's temporary polling
station. A word to tease her with,
taking a selfie standing near

an electric fence, a small herd of Polled
Herefords, curious enough to amble
closer, to see what the reflection
of themselves is about. To see
if I have a handful of grain

to feed them. Not that a handful
would add to their weight-in-the-world.
Would do anything more than delay their
turning away. For less time than it takes her
to message me to do anything

one person can do. To see inside a thousand
backpacks and briefcases walking by her.
To know what she doesn't,
she wouldn't have any way of knowing.
She could use the hive mind of her friends,

her Facebook friends. A corporate name,
a stanza ago, I was reluctant to use.
Until one of you posted for both of us
to look up from our phones. To see that
package synching at your feet.

Tracking Forgiveness

Stevens wrote *The imperfect is*
our paradise. Some days paradise is all
we have. A sentence

to live by. A therapist says
we're allowed to make twelve mistakes
a day. What's forgiveness for,

if not to set our watches by?
I wear Christ on my wrist
and have a hard time believing

everything Stevens wrote.
Remember he was an underwriter
who wrote poems and insurance

policies. I want to make as many mistakes
as I can in my lifetime.
So I can be my own actuary, sign

Perfection's policy. My wife says
I shouldn't have left the bird feeder out
for a bear to trash last night,

to leave his tracks in the hungry snow.
Says she married me so we can live
in paradise.

I've made it a habit of waking up

and walking in the morning.
Letting rain and snow, the falling
temperature, begin each day

with their own predictable
surprises. Overnight bobcat
tracks. A coat, frost-heavy,

draped over a mailbox.
The sense everything and nothing's
the same, going out, coming back.

Particularly the invisible wild
turkeys, who seem to make
a point of leaving a semblance

of themselves in a few feathers
released as signs on the road.
Where, it appears, they unknowingly

point a way into the woods.
As if you and I can make as much
as we need to of their absence.

Of flying without flying.
Hiding in the empty branches.
Not to make a poem

of this image too quickly.
The turkeys a tree protects
from the wind. From the memory

of a neighbor dreaming in his forest.
Another image I'm not sure
a poem is ready to save.

Ready to save a second way of saying
ready to keep. To write down and, one
morning, eventually, to type.

To Your Perpetrator

I'd mail him a valentine
of knives, if I knew
where he lived. A box

of heart-shaped
snakes. I'd be his UPS
man, deliver chocolate

nails and napalm lace.
An unsigned card
of threats, greeting him

each time his doorbell
rang. I'd burn a ring
of cinnamon around his

perpetrating house. Dare him
to mow his grass, I'd plant
with IEDs, a father's homemade

tripped device. I'd
devise for him for his
deliverance. Tripping

all over me.
I'd be so in his face.
Eye to eye. Tooth to tooth.

Love being the place I'd bite into.
No Christ of red
forgiveness.

Heaven

That first night it's likely you won't be able
to sleep. More like renting a room in a motel
and trying to guess what a sound means

in the next room. If she's kept against
her will. If the occupant forgot to turn off
his TV. Here, sound's an eternity

of gasps and moans. Of making as much
as you can of a rented bed. And having
to decide to call 911, to have the clouds

break down a door. To see what's happening.
Even when it's too early to think
in familiar terms. On night one.

When you haven't put away your things yet.
When no one knows where you are.
For whose sake. Or if you're where

you thought you'd be.
Trying to fall asleep. Hoping to read
that blinking NO VACANCY sign.

Constitution

When I bump into my friend Steve this morning,
he doesn't hesitate to tell me he and his new wife will
enjoy a late breakfast at The Bridge in Addison, Vermont,

near Lake Champlain. Enjoy the names
on the plastic menu, for battles and one fish
resembling the story of the native Vermonter

whose line became tangled in an endless
monster. Whose tale is told whenever the ferry's
crossing. This morning, after their Ethan Allen

omelet and Redcoat coffee, Steve says he and his
bride will walk over the water by way of the new
bridge spanning the story. Tying two states

together over The Narrows. Where the dead
can be counted. Shipwrecks and drowned
flags. Where a fish appears to be a monster

to any couple out walking, celebrating a first
long marriage and this one. Steve says will last,
as long as there's a Revolutionary name

for eggs and bacon, pancakes and sausage,
onions and peppers, home fries and reenacted
maple syrup, a cook calls The Constitution.

Ending the Rumor

Shelf-stocker, fruit-stacker, meat-cutter,
sandwich-maker, bread-deliverer, mostly
women-at-the-registers, after-hours floor-

sweeper, beer men, carton-cutters, teenage
part-time workers, past and present
owners, behind-the-deli-glass caterers

catering to their neighbors, to passing-through
travelers, middle-of-the-night
truck drivers, here, by the train's stopping,

the engineer leaving his Vermont
Railway engine idling, running in
for what-used-to-be-free coffee, his saved

newspaper, some early morning talking.
Call it conversation and not about
the store-closing.

3

Calendar of Leaves

November's a leafless feeling.
Don't think there's anyone
who hasn't felt this. Say
grief's a universal, selfish feeling.

Whoever said any month is a month
for grieving wasn't kidding. Was plain
speaking. Knew how numb
you feel as the year turns

over its new leaf, making impossible
promises. I was foolish
to think you'd live beyond your
keeping. Long life doesn't promise

anything. A new month. A moon
feeling like a calendar
of leaves,
a page of branches.

Assisted Living

I would have wanted a nicer view
for you. Instead of this wall, outside
your door, raised to mute

the road. To keep
the coyotes at bay. Wanted a bird-of-
paradise to split the concrete.

So you could see its latest blooming.
Even the flower doesn't know why
it's here. For whom

it was meant to be. Only that it rises
beyond itself. Beyond any desire.
Useless now, for me to think

you could've used more space,
for more than a dresser and a bed,
two chairs for visitors. One

or none at all. Save for the night
nurse who'll need to get off
her feet. Who will sit there for me,

the miles between us
what they are. Too much time
and space. A universe of shining

regret. All that I have to remember
tonight. The hall between our rooms.
Where we grew up. The train across

the road we couldn't see.
Peonies bursting
against the house.

The last time we didn't talk

I was sitting by your bed, watching you
move your lips. I could see there was

a breeze high in the palm leaves.
As if the leaves were speaking for you.
As if the freeway, beyond your door,

said what you would say.
If a few words could rise
in your throat, make their way

beyond your mouth.
I had to imagine with my heart
what it was you might have been

saying to me, what a sister would
say to her brother, the whispers of leaves
shaking each other. Below, the clouds

opening, leaving room for a sentence
of sky to write itself across both of
our minds. Our thoughts, racing

and still. Too fast, I want to say now,
when the only thing left is what
we might have said in your going.

The silence we'll keep to ourselves.
And the palm trees swaying.
All that noise jamming the freeways.

Lowering You

It's possible you're listening,
as they lower you into the ground
to our mother. Even this far
away, I have to imagine you still
make quite a pair. Your bouffant

coiffed hair. Eyes lined,
looking into death's instant camera.
The Polaroid, that died
its own death, giving way
to a new model of itself. That,

so quickly, shows you yourself.
Looking up, listening to the words
the grave men have found a way
for me to say what I can. My words
crumbling, as they lower you down

to her. One of their phones they
use as a speaker, tied to a string,
that's held over you. So I have
to believe you both might hear
the prayer I'm speaking on speaker-

phone. Words our father, buried
over there by the freeway's drone,
would have to uncover his ears
to hear. If only he could still
listen. To any echoing word.

4

Please don't thank me

for the three months
I served, stateside, in barracks
more like a dorm than a hooch.

When my friends were overseas,
sleeping in rain and blood. For more
than a year. Some of them returned

to less than a canteen of thanks.
A few said, *Don't feel guilty.*
What good would that do?

Even if I remember the base
I trained on in San Antonio.
The burned and grafted taking

their morning walks.
Grateful to be there and not in
a thankless paddy. A Huey

chopping the air, taking too long
to land. To lift them. Past
please and *thank you*. Words

we were taught to save us.
I can't thank you enough for not
thanking me for my service.

Love Beyond Us and the Falling

Perhaps our love can save the memory
of our government. The night we remember
to lie in the grass and even the voles aren't afraid

to vote for us and not one of their own.
Aren't trapped, running in circles not meant
for them. We promise not to forget the thought

of each other and the feeling of happiness.
Even when the field changes its mind
and we believe it instead of ourselves.

We're two grains in a granary. Small
and vast. And willing to undress in sight
of the sun. To make love anywhere

there's a chance of victory. Of taking
ourselves into account.
Of laying down our lives

for an empty flag. Remembering
how long we can survive without
touching, believing in love beyond us

and the falling stars. Beyond thinking
there's another election inside
your eyes and mine.

On the Lift

There's not a better place
on earth than sitting
with Bill McKibben

in County Tire's waiting room.
Our cars hoisted on lifts.
Two men behind

the glass, swapping out
sets of tires. Balancing them
with weights from fishing

lines, the balance
bubbles showing our wait's
almost over. Although

with the clouds gathering,
the temperature dropping,
it may be better to pray

the snow's staying away
for one more swapped day.
To let the plows stay

where they are
in the town shed.
Salt and sand rising

into a mountain again.
The roads clear and no
black ice, no freaky snowstorm

we could have predicted.
I don't have to say anything
more about to Bill.

How we go about saving
the earth, one-season-to-the-next,
winter-to-spring tires.

Downton's Last Lawn

With four episodes left, the writer
leaves it to us to guess who Lady
Mary will let fall in love with her.
A former lover? A man, a woman still
to be unveiled? Perhaps the groomed

lawn, nature being the lover
that it is. Foreshadowed in Season
Three, when Mary, leaning in,
seemed to kiss the water
in the fountain. Saw her own,

another's rippling reflection.
Leaving us to see it wasn't just sex
she was after, after all her survived
disasters. Wasn't putting love
ahead of running the class-crumbling

manor. Or gender. A word not
invented yet for them. Although there's
really no confusion as to what the men do
and the women. Although the writer knows
her history to write into a script's changes.

To leave it to us to guess who, what Lady
Mary will end up with. Loneliness, a camera
panning over Downton Abbey? You and I
not knowing what we'll have to do now
on Sunday evenings.

Not Refusing Them

I could call that boy,
in his father's arms at the prow
of the raft, a head-scarfed

Odysseus. Say the wrong word
for what they're doing.
Not *disembarking*.

But jumping, knee-deep,
into the thrashing Lesbos sea.
The island, one stone to step on,

to take them where they're going.
Too many of them
for that boat to carry.

Its maximum number erased.
And who's taking their lifetime
of money. So they can live in a tented,

permanent shelter, speak
a new language.
His father's holding a sign

POET AND PLUMBER.
Hoping he'll be discovered,
they'll be waved onto a ship

in German. They can walk off
and not into deportation's
water.

Visiting Poet

No one told me I'd be sitting
across the table from Deyanira, number
two wife of Hercules, the name her parents

assigned her. Sitting in her classroom
at the foot of Grass Mountain,
a dry Olympus. Where the gods

wear masks of spiders and snakes,
the dead drum their Chumash bones.
No one gave me a heads-up, across the road

fans still drive to the gates
of Neverland. To leave notes to his
ghost, love's allegations.

Everything that he did there.
Isn't a poem where we name what was done?
Where a goddess can be saved

by a god from rape? Blood's
a river, even in this drought.
I want to assign you a line you can

dream, then write.
Bring to class tomorrow
when I'm gone. Imagine you were

named for a goddess like Deyanira,
gazing out the window. Thinking
of that boy across the road

writing his note to Michael,
hat-tilted, one-gloved, dancing
his moonwalk.

Returning to the Counseling Center

It doesn't take long to remember you
once worked here. Listened to redwings

singing, scratching their throats. Reading
the body language of branches. And later

writing your clinical notes. Diagnostic
codes for a swan who didn't want

to leave her room.
The wind who knew he was a girl

who couldn't be coded. It's hard to forget
you sat by a window looking out

toward the mountains. Its shades
of light, its seasons of faces. Whenever

you too felt discouraged. Not knowing
when listening makes a difference or how

long it takes for a swan to step out
of her room, a girl to forsake the wind.

There are many stories of branches,
professional and personal notes. To leave,

to take with you. To fill in the spaces.
To recall the widening circles

of water, those students who were
patient with you.

Easter's Ginsberg and Corso

I moved ahead, eager to rejoin old company . . .
I went to the movie of my life.
Allen Ginsberg

I'm reminded this day before Christ
rose, Gregory Corso invited my friend
Peter and me to drive him to Ginsberg's

and Orlovsky's farm, downstate,
for Allen's birthday. Peter lived in a commune
with Gregory in Buffalo.

Where that poet was loving his methadone
and heroin. Two lines in his high
poem. The one he promised he'd write

on the drive down. If only we could
see our way past what we'd find.
Men sitting around a dining room

table, waiting for Gregory to arrive,
rise with them. Once Allen began playing
his harmonium, breathing life with his feet

into its canvas lungs. Raising his voice,
no one would call singing, really.
If you weren't stoned on love,

men's love. Peter and I—am I remembering
right?—espoused in the abstract. Seeking
advice, in those days, from the I Ching,

those pictographs of sticks and stones,
their random messaging. Should we stay,
should we go? Wondering if we could stand

listening to our backseat poet, droning
for hours on the thruway. Driving
our crystal Christ, wearing a shawl

and his court jester shoes, their tips curled.
Gregory said Allen would have him
take off at the door. Said Peter and I could leave

our clothes on, when the dancing began.
When, he wanted us to know,
there'd be more than one Christ

rising, coming down. Even if we left
the car running all weekend, by the private
gate. If we'd be there to drive him home.

Retiring, really?

He says he's retiring at the end
of the year. A year's a season.
He's so well-seasoned, Boston's
Dominican. Swinging for the fences.

Where a fence is a wall
monster. Some nights he's all
smiles. Some days he bares
his teeth. This bear

of a Dominican.
We'll be lost without his swing.
I don't want to think of him
kicking back, polishing his bling.

Although he deserves everything
coming to him. A wind
blowing out to left. A designated,
lifetime fan. I like to think of myself

as one of his record-breaking, going,
going, gone statistics. Almost Spanish-
speaking. Spitting into the palms
of my gloved hands. Stepping

into a chalked dirt box. And
with one flip of my bat—
call it his wand, *su varita*—
it's gone again, leaving the park,

that ball driven from the big man,
retiring itself for the two of us.
Let's retire his number
but not his name. And that

breeze blowing out
to right, to Ortiz's bullpen.
Who said, after the bombing,
This is our fucking city.

Are You a Poet or an End?

Who would you be in the moment
  the ball's tipped into your sudden hands?
When you've been coached to leave thinking

behind, practiced those given routes.
  When suddenly is what the game's about.
And your hands, soft

as a retriever's mouth. Isn't an end
  whistle-trained not to bring back a ball.
To take it, an announcer says, *to the house*.

A zone you'd like to live in at the end
  of a game. Surprising yourself at what hours,
late in the afternoon, can come to.

When you were tired of what
  you had to do like a machine,
on command. Run out. Cut right. Trust

the ball will be there. On time.
  Love what you'll find in your hands.
Love the safety who made a mistake.

Chagall's Girl

I'm assigned to sit next to the new girl
from Iraq, to teach her elementary school
English. I didn't volunteer to point

to things and say their words.
It's 1954 again.
There are names for things I can

point to, in and out of school.
My friends look at me as if I'm
the traitor I am. I begin to like her

sooner. Holding her hand on the yellow
paper. I can tell she thinks three letters
make a bird, this girl from her former

land. She asks me if I know
the word for *magic*. Showing me
her wings at recess beneath her blouse.

My friends don't understand. Threaten
to never speak to me again.
I'm too young not to believe in

threats and *Shorbat Rumman,*
her mother's pomegranate soup,
she brings for me in her *thermos*.

That *chalice* holding hot and cold.
Two words I didn't know I knew.
Until she rose. As if she were one

of Chagall's girls, rising over
her hometown, smoking village.
As if those curling leaves

were notes. And not her father
yelling to her from the parking lot. Not
my friends, taunting her their love.

Museum of Islands

At my age, my friends say I'd better get out
and travel when I can, before time
takes its toll at the toll gate. Before the last

national park is closed. And the airlines stop
letting me preboard. Sit closer
to a World War II pilot, who's close

to giving up his wings. Landing
a few minutes ahead of time.
Friends tell me to attack

my bucket list. A map of places that want
to see me before I forget where to go.
The sun shimmering a river. A mom-

and-pop store, off the road, known
for its early-morning cider donuts.
And early morning. When, lying in bed,

I can forget how old I am, scroll through
pictures of where my friends have been.
The museum of islands. A palace

of rented rooms. A rock overlooking
a sea, they say, hasn't been named yet
and is waiting for me. To book a reservation

with all the miles I haven't frequented.
To step out my front door with my right
foot, my father assured me would keep me

safe. Whenever I thought I was going away.
Whenever he said not to worry,
if he didn't return on time.

Acknowledgments

The author gratefully acknowledges these magazines, newspapers and media for the publication, posting and presentation of the poems in this book, sometimes in earlier versions.

Addison Independent
Facebook
Loft Anthology: New England Poetry and Art
Massachusetts Review
Middlebury Magazine
Roads Taken: Contemporary Vermont Poetry
Somerville Times
Vermont Public Radio: Downton Abbey Gala Program
Vox Populi

Open this book up on any page and you'll find a line, a phrase, a stanza, a poem that jumps out at you. I did. There are poems here that will line the walls of your subconscious and keep you company for a long while to come.

—CALVIN FORBES, author of *Blue Monday* and *From the Book of Shine*

These poems are full of a kind of urgent benevolence, in which the world is constantly revising itself. Perhaps no other writer has gotten so much out of the word "or"—a sort of prelude to an exfoliation of possibilities, of promising variants, constituting a magnificent affirmation that "there's more than one way / to be in the world." Or the piling up of infinitives, each one catapulting us onto a different plane of being. Or the syntax, the dependent clauses which have shaken off their fetters, so that they can cross-pollinate every sentence, every image, every possibility in the poem. I love it that red-winged blackbirds haunt these poems, along with baseball, teaching, and counseling (including a moving section about working with prisoners), the state of the world, the wonders of Vermont. I wonder if any poet since Whitman has invited us so irresistibly into his cosmos (and himself into ours).

—JOHN PLANT, composer of *I will fly like a bird*

At the center of Gary Margolis's poems is the human, the head, reconciling with the swirling, radiant natural world it confronts: the planetary body. Like Dante wandering the underworld, so Margolis wanders, but deeply grounded on our living landscape. Some poems turn from praise to grim acknowledgment, pointing out war and human conflict's effects, but always with an element of hope. These poems are like "A bird trying to sing itself back to you" as well, allowing the possibility of "Imagining the day / we'd walk down a street, / arm in arm with our enemies." It is a collection of reconciliation and witness; solidarity with the writer and the naturalist. In this New & Selected, we see the breadth of Margolis's skills as a writer, which are as sharp and ecstatic as ever.

—BIANCA STONE, author of *The Möbius Strip Club of Grief*